Contents

Foreword

Dennis Littky

You are about to read a book about an exciting place: the New Country School (NCS). These essays will help you understand the philosophy behind the school, as well as other people's thinking and research to connect it all together.

It was a wonderfully confirming experience for me to read the book, because we at The Big Picture Company have started a school called the Met, in Providence, R.I., along with twenty-five more that follow a similar philosophy.

There are not many schools like the Minnesota New Country School and the Big Picture schools in this country, so when something is written about them it's important to read.

The beauty of this book is that it runs the gamut from getting the feel for passionate people meeting after work to design a school to the research and philosophy behind the construction of these schools. There are a lot of examples outside of the New Country School that support the work being done there.

The book, the schools, and the stories make so much sense. No classroom, no bells, no textbooks. We don't have these things in our everyday learning, so why in schools? In life, we set our own times for how long tasks take. We work wherever it is most appropriate and our reference material is usually not a textbook. The description of NCS shows us how the real goals of learning are teaching students how to learn and how to manage their lives. The provided writing by these students will show you what they have accomplished.

Throughout all the good practice and philosophy at NCS is the fact that teachers organize themselves into a cooperative and become the owners of instructional services rather than employees of the school. This is a very different way to run schools.

The fact that faculty and students get to practice democracy rather than just read about it is another strong point of NCS. In reading the book, you'll feel the struggles of the staff and students. You'll feel the hard work and understand that creating a great school is not magic. You'll see how trust had to be first be developed.

Then there are the corresponding essays that go deep into research and philosophy. It's a good feeling to read about the school, feel it, and believe in it in your gut and then have research and references to support your gut feeling. You'll get a quick summary of the literature (Barth, Kohl, Schwab, Piaget, Adler, Kropotkin, Wheatley, Cuban, Dewey, etc.) in the context of real practice.

Some of these authors you know and have read, and others will be new to you. The book will give you the opportunity to broaden your background and gain knowledge necessary to strengthening your work. This is a must-read: we must all understand and know about schools that have been successful while at the same time being very different; we must understand that these schools are based on solid theory and research; we must use these schools as starting points and points of comparison; and we must publicize these schools to help push our thinking.

I thank the editors and contributors (the writing was, of course, a democratic, joint venture) for writing *The Coolest School in America*.

Introduction

Ron Newell

PART 1: THE FOUNDING AND DEVELOPMENT OF THE MINNESOTA NEW COUNTRY SCHOOL

The first five chapters of this book are about the birth and development of a very unique school, one that has obtained a great deal of notoriety in America and abroad. This school, in a little town in rural Minnesota, has gained this notoriety because the founders took reform to a level not often seen in education. The school has no classrooms, no bells, and no textbooks; the people who work at the school are not employees of the school; the building in which it is housed was not directly built with public dollars; students work at their own pace and are not graded; graduation is by competence and performance through creating projects as well as meeting standards; and students decide how, when, where, and what to study. For these reasons the school has been called "the coolest school in America" by Tom Vander Ark of the Bill and Melinda Gates Foundation, and they are why the foundation selected the school as a model to be replicated across America.

That coolest school is the Minnesota New Country School (MNCS), located in Henderson, Minnesota (population 1,000). The school has never had more than 125 students from ten or more area districts, with 40 percent or so from the local sponsoring district. They come together to create a unique and effective learning community. The school began in 1994 and has graduated eight to sixteen students per year since. Graduates do well.

They are taught how to manage their own lives by developing life skills. In other words, they are taught *how* to learn.

The first part of this book is about the development of that school. The founders of the school did not create it to start a national reform movement. They simply wanted students to become purposeful adults, not be subjected to the subtle and not so subtle forces that generally antagonize adolescents. The school was about a different form of teaching: facilitating and guiding the acquisition of knowledge, as opposed to delivering a curriculum. It was about advisory groups that create a family-like atmosphere; it was about student workstations, just like in the real world; and it was about students having real-world experiences using the whole world as the curriculum.

The founders of the school not only developed a new way of educating high school students; they also created a new kind of teacher organization. Organized into a professional practice around a cooperative legal structure, EdVisions Cooperative allowed teachers to sell their "intellectual capital" and services to the school and the parents. In return, they have control of the learning program, the hiring and retention of personnel, and most of the budget, and they are responsible for the success of the school. This alternative management system is as futuristic an element of the endeavor as is the learning program.

PART 2: BUILDING THE LEARNING COMMUNITY

In the past three or four years, a number of great thinkers and doers have become associated with EdVisions. These friends and colleagues, oftentimes hired as consultants, have contributed greatly to the development of the refined methods and to the replication efforts. And we continue to learn from all of them. The second part of this book is made up of essays by many of those friends and coworkers. We have learned much from them, and they have learned from the school staff and students over the years. Compiling the knowledge of these great thinkers and doers around the story of the development of MNCS and other sites only makes sense. Placing together all we have learned about a different form of schooling and a powerful way of learning will prove to be instructive and useful to others about to embark on the journey.

PART 3: SOME RESULTS OF THE LEARNING COMMUNITIES

This book also includes chapters that describe what can happen when a learning community is formed. The first chapter studies MNCS graduates from the first five years of the school. Another chapter tells about the development of a school constitution developed by students and staff. A third contains quotes from students and parents about being members of learning communities based on the MNCS model. Many voices speak to why these learning communities are indeed "cool" places to be. By 2004, fifteen schools, using some elements of project-based learning and teacher management, are affiliated with EdVisions. There are five or six more schools using the model, although not officially a part of the network. These unique learning environments are believed to be, by those students who attend them, the "coolest schools in America."

We ask that interested parties read this book and learn in a few hours what it took many of us a lifetime to learn. If these reflections, ideas, and thoughts inspire you to want to learn more, three other books published by ScarecrowEducation can help: *Teachers as Owners*, edited by Ed Dirkswager; *Passion for Learning*, by Ronald J. Newell; and *Democratic Learning and Leading*, by Ronald J. Newell and Irving H. Buchen.

It took ten years for the coolest schools in America to come to maturity, and it has been an exciting journey for all involved. Many teachers and students have found success in EdVisions schools. The journey, therefore, has been rewarding. We hope that you will start your own journey on the shoulders of those who were unafraid of the future.

Part 1

THE FOUNDING AND DEVELOPMENT OF THE MINNESOTA NEW COUNTRY SCHOOL

The following four chapters are about the beginning of a little school that has developed into a national model for project-based learning and democratic governance. It is from this foundation that others have learned that it is possible to change everything about education.

1

Little Did We Know

Doug Thomas

It's been ten years now since a group of educators and community members met in the Minnesota River Valley southwest of Minneapolis to create a new and unique secondary school. Equipped with all the latest reports and pushed by some better-known national reformers, they set out to be one of the first schools to challenge and change everything about high school — the learning program, the daily schedule, the calendar, the facility, governance, and the role of the educator. In challenging almost all conventional thinking around secondary education and school governance, particularly during a period of retrenchment in experimentation and innovation, the resulting school has received an uncommon amount of attention.

The planners were not your typical education experts. They were classroom teachers, aspiring administrators, board members, former board members, and frustrated ex-teachers. One was a meat cutter by trade and another a bricklayer. A few had been teacher–mentors through a unique program at Minnesota State University–Mankato. Not one had a published article, nor had any of them been keynote speakers at any school reform conferences. Their common bond was a good deal of experience with high school students and frustration at the lack of creative energy and rigor demonstrated in their respective schools. They were ready for big changes.

They met for a year in bars and coffee shops, the group expanding and waning with the busy-ness of its members. Their beginning premise was

3

to examine what was not working well for students in traditional high schools. They paid close attention to students rather than teachers and administrators. They knew well that too many decisions had been made to satisfy everyone other than students. After the year of planning, influenced by reading Ted Sizer, Myles Horton, and Peter Senge and being counseled by others like Joe Nathan, Wayne Jennings, and Ted Kolderie, they had little left that looked like the schools they knew. The resulting design plan and a supportive school board and superintendent helped them win one of the state's first charter school contracts in 1994.

Not without its detractors, the proposed school planners faced the typical response from those who are part of the current monopoly. Accusations of potential "creaming" of students and predictions of financial ruin for the local school (neither of which ever happened) were heard by the board of education. A series of hearings allowed everyone to vent and the planners to explain their reasons for attempting to create such a different high school. Keep in mind that this is in the heart of rural, southern Minnesota, where test scores have always been quite good and, as Garrison Keillor says, "all the kids are above average."

Eventually, it was the board chair, Virginia Miller, and the superintendent, Harold Larson, who spoke eloquently in support of choices and innovation. As a member of that board, it still gives me goosebumps to recall the night we gave the final go-ahead for the Minnesota New Country School. After receiving sponsorship from the local district, the Minnesota State Board of Education chartered the school as the seventh charter school in the state, making the Minnesota New Country School one of the first 100 charter schools in the nation.

That momentous decision in a relatively small district (1,500 students) still addresses and questions the institutional heritage of public education across America. What does it mean to be "public" in America today? Does a local public school board have to "own" all the public schools within its boundaries? Can someone else provide the service of public education within the geographic and political jurisdiction of another state-authorized and state-sanctioned entity? How should the public be taxed to pay for its education programs? Could teachers and parents run their own schools without the usual bureaucratic oversight? Could high schools be successful without courses? We knew some of the questions we were addressing but had no idea of their policy implications and importance. Furthermore, we were ahead of the curve in terms of assessment and accountability, using a learning program that would require an entirely different assessment system. More ground broken.

The New Country School program really did change almost everything for secondary students. As a part of our planning, each week we would tackle another familiar component of typical schooling. One week it was the daily schedule, another considered whether we needed bells, and yet another considered whether we should have a principal. In the end, we had little left that looked like regular school. We eliminated courses as a way of dividing and framing the curriculum. We went with a distributive, teacher–leader model of daily governance. With the elimination of courses, we no longer needed bells, hallway passing, lavatory passes, class schedules, study halls, and all the other things that came along with a more rigid, time-based system.

We changed the calendar so students could work well into the summer and so the advisers could include biking, hiking, canoeing, and camping trips. We tried to put a personal computer on every student's desk so they would be linked to the Internet at any time. And we created a competency and assessment system where students would present their work for validation every six weeks at a community presentation night.

The New Country School has become a lighthouse for progressive approaches to standards-driven school programming. Looking like a larger version of a one-room schoolhouse (125 students), the school is located in Henderson, approximately sixty miles southwest of Minneapolis. In some ways, it is a throwback to the old days of education. The students are of mixed ages and grades, all moving at their own pace and choosing topics of interest. Yet the high-tech environment and the attention to modern standards define a more contemporary style of accountability and attention to personalization. Their ability to weave the standards into self-directed student projects has become a hallmark of the school.

The difficulty in providing rigor took a couple of years to overcome, but once the articulation of standards and projects was accomplished, a certain settling in took place in the building, and there was far less wandering by students and wondering by advisers. The chaos of the early months was replaced by a more serious attention to quality and organization.

At the same time that students were adjusting, the educators were experiencing a radical transformation. For the first time in public education, teachers organized themselves into a cooperative and became the owners of the instructional services rather than employees of the school. It was a worker's cooperative applied to a professional setting. This unique model put the teachers in control of the learning program, compensation, and professional development.

Because the teachers chose not to hire a typical administrator, they also were providing site leadership. They did so with a distributive leadership model, each of the educators joining two committees and essentially becoming experts in at least one area of school operations. The committees consist of finance, transportation, curriculum, personnel, special education, student records and reporting, and food service.

The ownership of the learning program added an additional level of accountability and brought a greater level of entrepreneurship to the undertaking. Teachers could no longer feel they were serving the will of an administrator or reacting to typical micromanaging by the school board. They were directly responsible for the success or failure of the school. The board's role changed dramatically as well. It took on four primary functions: entering into agreements (contracts, of which the cooperative contract was one), taking care of facilities, establishing policies, and looking for results. They no longer got involved in minor personnel issues, worried about daily student problems, or second-guessed teaching strategies. Issues with program and personnel were taken to the EdVisions Cooperative and addressed by the contract.

The idea of a teacher professional practice, organized as a cooperative, adds an equity notion to the organization. Cooperatives are a fairly common and acceptable business model in the rural Midwest. Applying the model to public education was something quite different. A recent book on the idea, *Teachers as Owners* (Dirkswager 2002), was written by a group of Minnesota educators and policymakers. EdVisions now serves nine other schools and over 125 teachers and at-large members. Evaluation and recruitment services have been added to the offerings of the cooperatives.

The facility also has taken on the look of a modern one-room schoolhouse. It looks more like a busy office than a typical school. Every student has a personal work space, most equipped with a personal computer. The students are grouped in an advisory, each adviser (teacher) being responsible for the learning program of fifteen to eighteen students, grades

7 to 12. The adviser groups are essentially in a large, open space the center of which contains tables for group work, enough space to seat 250 people for larger events, and a stage (with a Harvestore silo backdrop) to accommodate presentations.

There are several rooms off this open space. One is a science lab and greenhouse, another is the media resource center and quiet study area, another is the art and shop project area, and two smaller rooms serve as the special education room. Total square footage is 17,000, or 136 square feet per student. There is a large park behind the school for outdoor activities, a public library three blocks away, and community recreation center and gymnasium four miles away. Students are bused to the recreation center for such activities as racquetball, swimming, weight lifting, and skating.

Just as important is how the school building came about. Minnesota public charter schools can own buildings, but public funding is restricted in such cases. However, lease aid is provided on a per-pupil basis. Therefore, most charter school buildings are owned by developers or nonprofit groups. In Henderson, a unique partnership was created to develop the school building. Several Main Street business owners and other interested and supportive parties wanted the school to locate in downtown Henderson. They pooled their resources and came up with the down payment on the $1.2 million facility.

In addition, the City of Henderson, with county assistance, provided tax increment financing to purchase and improve the property, a local bank made available the balance needed for construction, and the U.S. Department of Agriculture backed the loan through its Rural Development Loan Guarantee Program. In essence, it became a small-town economic development success story and an interesting public–private partnership. A private development group seeded the project, the local community helped with infrastructure, a local bank contributed financing (supported by a federal agency), and the state-level program provides the sustaining funds. The ownership group has since converted to nonprofit status and is planning an addition to the school using the state's lease-hold improvement program and financing from the National Cooperative Bank.

After nearly ten years, the school and cooperative are thriving. But it doesn't seem to be any less work. As a "disruptive innovation," we shouldn't expect to ever settle into much of a routine. Some of us have ventured into the replication work. The Bill and Melinda Gates Foundation has generously placed its faith in us to create new versions of the New Country School and EdVisions Cooperative. In just over two years, we have marshaled the creation of a dozen more schools in Minnesota and Wisconsin and, with further assistance from the Gates Foundation, are about to launch a national effort to create twenty more.

REFERENCE

Dirkswager, E., ed. (2002). *Teachers as owners: A key to revitalizing American education*. Lanham, MD: ScarecrowEducation, 2002.

2

Putting Ideas to Work

Doug Thomas

What brought the EdVisions Cooperative folks together, and what has carried their torch since the fall of 1992? They were a set of beliefs and practices that have been well researched and supported but rarely all used as the cornerstones of an entire school. I was aware of many of these ideas independently, but to put them all together is something quite extraordinary. Some of them are deeply embedded in the essence of a speech I remember from 1994 given by Joe Nathan, director of the Center for School Change at the Humphrey Institute, University of Minnesota. Nathan probably got it from Herb Kohl and Ted Sizer. They probably got it from Don Glines and James Conant. And somebody down the line must have gotten it from John Dewey. Joe Nathan told the group that there are six elements that most excite and motivate students:

- Education takes place out of the school building.
- Students really want to do it and have a choice in what they pursue.
- Students have an opportunity to collaborate with others.
- Students produce something. There is some product and an audience beyond the teacher.
- Students' efforts are useful to other people.
- Students have an opportunity for reflection and refinement.

Essentially, we've tried to implement all six of these at the New Country School and other schools. In many traditional schools, you will see one or two of these elements or all of them used only occasionally. I try to convince teachers everywhere that if they do all these on a consistent basis, they will have a very different and exciting kind of school. They are simple notions and certainly not the only strategies to employ in schools, but they can produce some powerful results. You'll recognize some of them in our basic philosophy.

First, we believe in choice. We are a group that recognized choices for nearly every facet of our society except schools. Education has become a monoculture, and we are determined to offer something extraordinary. Minnesota has led the nation in policies to allow students and parents to choose from a variety of optional programs and schools. We appreciated these opportunities but also recognized that choices are only as good as the distinction they offer. We needed more and different kinds of schools, especially the more student-centered, integrated curriculum type of programs for high schools.

The public has grown accustomed to having choices in schools. A recent independent survey commissioned by the Center for School Change at the University of Minnesota found that 75 percent of Minnesota parents favor the ability to choose the public schools their children attend. With various other programs (charters, postsecondary options, magnets, at-risk programs, and so on) alongside open enrollment, it is not out of the ordinary for one family to use several options.

It is our observation that traditional high schools work great for a number of students. Our rough estimate is that 20 to 30 percent really like or will thrive in traditional high schools. Another 30 to 40 percent are bored or frustrated because of mismatched learning styles or lack of relevance but survive. And another 20 to 30 percent simply can't function in regular school because of a lack of basic skills, learning disabilities, belligerence, cultural issues, or deviant behavior. Many of that group are assigned to "at-risk" schools or simply drop out. As Tom Vander Ark from the Bill and Melinda Gates Foundation explains, "We lose 3,500 students every day in this country. Of the incoming eighth graders each year in America, five million of the seven million will either drop out or be unprepared for productive work or postsecondary education as they leave high school. It's a national tragedy." We agree that this is simply unacceptable. We must meet the needs of more students by offering more options and opportunities for success.

Second, we are committed to creating and sustaining excellent small schools. Small schools (under 250 students) work for a greater percentage of young people, and they create a sense of community that, ironically, is often not found in the real world anymore. Study after study is showing the benefits of smaller learning communities. Many families are seeking smaller learning environments because they want to be more involved and want a more personalized relationship with teachers and other families. All the planners of the New Country School had a similar notion about school size, partly because of our own educational experiences and partly because of our collective research in creating the school.

Our intention at the New Country School and our replication schools has been to keep schools under 200 students and when possible stay in the range of 100 to 150. This seems to be the desired number in order to facilitate advisory groups and allow the physical space to be manageable. In addition, we've found that small schools of this fashion are very efficient when a team of teachers provide the leadership. Schools of more than 200 students seem to require a principal or some kind of discipline personnel and often develop a less-than-personal climate. Our ultimate goal was always to create a school based more on personal relationships with students and less on control rules that made it easier for the adults. We had all seen far too much of that in larger schools.

Vander Ark says that "class size makes all the difference in elementary schools and school size makes all the difference in secondary schools." One of the many confounding contemporary notions is this move to larger and larger high schools over the past century and especially the past thirty years. We have an "edifice complex" that has led policymakers and school officials to be fascinated with larger schools at the expense of our student's health and wellness, even to the point of death (witness Columbine). What kind of society forsakes the safety of its children for this depersonalized economy of scale?

Next, and going hand in hand with school size, is the well-proven but often misunderstood practice of service learning and civic learning. I use the word "practice" here because it is so applicable. We don't become good community members by osmosis. This is truly something we learn (and even at a young age) by doing. We believe wholeheartedly that learning in community fosters a love and respect for community and creates a civic responsibility that turns into positive activism later. It's how we learn democracy and how government works. And adolescents who know their communities and have a sense of place are less likely to be involved in destructive behavior.

Service learning fits very well with our project-based schoolwork as well. Students are searching for group and individual projects and need real work that can help other people. They are willing and able to help solve community problems, investigate issues, or help make improvements to their neighborhoods. They can also help with school governance and thereby learn valuable lessons in government and civic action. We tend to leave two large and productive segments out of our community and economic efforts: the young and the old. It's even more powerful when those two groups combine the wisdom of elders with youthful enthusiasm.

It's ironic for a country so reliant on its citizens to understand and appreciate democracy to have so little in practice in its public schools. Outside the mock student government in place, most schools are oligarchies or dictatorships. We've had at least a couple of generations that know little of the actual workings of active citizenship and democratic decision making. Throughout elementary and secondary school, most of the decisions are made for us. The transition from quality and accountability to democracy in this country is often lost in the premise that "I need to tell you what to do so you get it right" (no room for mistakes) and "We'd love for you to know this, but we don't have time, so we'll just do it for you" (somehow learning will take place later).

A logical extension of service learning is active, constructive learning. Touted by various progressive education groups for the past century and now being taught in teacher preparation programs more frequently, constructivist learning has been assailed to a certain degree over the decades. With the most recent "back to basics" and standardization, everyone has their right and wrong version of the best teaching methods. What always seems to be a political football to the adults is allowing something real for young people that they enjoy. Even the simplest learning pyramid wouldn't put an inactive, sitting-and-listening style of learning anywhere near the level of enjoyment and motivation students get from working with their hands, being outdoors, conducting experiments, acting in plays, or building models. Kids don't care if the conservatives or the liberals support it or not, they just want to be interested and engaged in what they are learning.

Most recently, support has grown for constructivist learning through brain research. Building or growing knowledge with the assistance of a skilled facilitator is recognized as lasting and exciting. Our friend Walter Enloe, who wrote a chapter in this book, conducts a modest example of this in his workshops. He places an object with which no one in the room is familiar in front of an audience. He then asks a series of questions: What does it look like? What might it be used for? With each question, the knowledge of the object grows until finally someone figures it out. It is a powerful learning experience and one that many teachers have never thought much about, even though they undoubtedly use constructive practices. Some of the best are constantly using constructivist methods. Think of the opportunities we miss when we come at school-based learning in only very traditional methods.

Sometimes people will ask, "Why didn't all that work in the open schools of the 1960s and 1970s?" My answer is that we had a lot of good intentions and much good work was accomplished then but that today we know a lot more about learning. We also didn't have as much organizational sense back then. And we didn't have the knowledge of how the brain works that we have today. There is a lot of good research supporting active learning, and we know how the brain reacts to such methods. In order to emphasize this, I'll tell one of my favorite stories.

I was visiting a small elementary school some years ago. I heard about this fellow's teaching style and wanted to check it out. I got to the school, and here was this class of first and second graders all outside bouncing balls. I got close and realized they were counting. I believe they were partnered up, and one was bouncing and the other was counting. It was obvious that the whole day was centered on bouncing balls. They had been all over the school and grounds working with various types of balls.

At one point the teacher even scaled a ladder and bounced a ball from the roof top. They had moved on to some sort of elementary physics lesson. It seemed that no matter from what height the ball was dropped, it always bounced the same number of times. The bounces were just bigger. Later they were back bouncing the balls and counting again, adding and subtracting, and so on. At one point the teacher bounced two balls at once and posed the question as to how the students would be able to count the bounces of both balls at the same time. After several attempts to solve this problem, one little guy said, "One side of my brain will count one ball, and the other side of my brain will count the other ball." Not the correct answer, but I know when I was in first grade my brain wasn't getting that kind of exercise! (I'll let you figure out the right answer.)

My point is that we know so many more effective and interesting active learning methods now than we did even ten years ago. If we practice them, we are bound to create better schools. If we fall back to only drill and practice, we'll lose more inquisitive little minds to television and computer screens simply for reasons of mental stimulation. I think we can learn and have fun!

Next on our list of reasons for creating a new kind of school has to do with our notions of assessment and learning. We were appalled by the lack of rigor and accountability in grading and assessing student work. The expectations for useless recall were way out of balance. We all agreed that grades and learning had little to do with each other beyond preparing for the next level of schooling. Kids already know this. It's taking adults a while longer.

Having done some reading and visiting schools using more performance assessment, we decided it made a whole lot more sense to approach this area with varying degrees of authentic assessment. We designed a system where all student work would essentially be a product or presentation, judged by a team of teachers, peers, and sometimes community experts and parents. Credit toward standards would be awarded by multiple measures influenced by those who would find the work most useful. For example, if a student was validating his or her auto mechanical ability, it made sense to present that project to a certified local auto mechanic if possible.

Approximately every six weeks, our school holds a presentation night where family and community members come to observe, watch, and listen to students present their learning. Part of the formal evaluation of student work comes from the assessment taking place at presentation night. Students take their projects more seriously, they get valuable practice speaking in public, the parents better understand the learning process, and the public knows the school is serious about academics and it builds community. The program is entirely run by students, adding further experience to the students' repertoire.

The culminating high school experience is the senior presentation. We have all wondered about the validity of the ceremonial graduation, the rite of passage that so many students don't find to be that motivating anymore. We wanted graduation to mean something extraordinary, so we designed an academic graduation: the senior exhibit. At the New Country School, every graduating senior is expected to present a major project to the public. The projects are in-depth, high-tech exhibits that take between 300 and 400 hours to research, document, and create. A team of advisers and evaluators, including two community experts, oversee the project process through several months of preparation. The final product is an important part of a graduate's right of passage. In some cases, as many people attend a student's senior presentation as might attend the graduation ceremony held a month to six weeks later. For many seniors, the exhibit becomes far more meaningful as evidence of the right to move beyond high school.

My favorite senior presentation story is heart-wrenching. A few years ago a young man came to the New Country School just before the year began. He was a sharp-looking, six-foot-five, 230-pound young man who looked like he should be playing linebacker for a Division I college. Much to the contrary, he was not ready for college. He told the staff he was about to enter his senior year at a large suburban high school, held nearly a B average, but couldn't read. He wanted to go to college but could not pass the Minnesota Basic Skills test in reading.

What the school did next is quite fascinating. Instead of dismissing the young man as incapable or having an unfixable problem, they treated him as someone who they were confident they could help once they knew how. Since they viewed themselves as general practitioners, they sought out a specialist. They sent the young man to a nearby college to be tested by a reading expert to determine what learning disability was contributing to his inability to read. The professor did the testing and sent along a "prescription" to the school. The student made learning to read and passing the state test his senior project. The school advisers filled the prescription, and five months later the student passed the reading Basic Skills Test with a 94 out of 100.

I attended the senior presentation of this young man, and it was quite moving. He described in detail how he, along with a teaching assistant at the school, taught himself to read in 688 hours. A month later he was the happiest graduate I have ever seen. The last I heard he was attending a college.

There are numerous other ways to authenticate students' work and learning, including audio- and videotaping student performances, validating service learning, and assessing arts and academic competitions. No matter what the setting, if we want young people to become lifelong learners, we must be more intentional about getting them in the habit of thinking about what they learn in all their activities and how they demonstrate that learning.

Early in the life of the New Country School, we made a big deal of the access to technology available to students. We even did a little marketing based on how students would have unlimited access to computers and how every project would somehow be connected to the Internet for research. We soon learned that it was a necessity and not a luxury for students. You can't create good schools without good technology these days. And it's a priority for students to have them when their work is so self-directed and creative and requires so much information storage and retrieval. Today, we try to make sure there are two computers for every two or three students. That's still way ahead of most classrooms, but anything less is simply not an option anymore.

We knew technology was important to our students and the success of the school, but as the first years rolled by, we began to look at the role of technology in different ways. Joe Graba, of the Education Evolving in St. Paul, began to refer to our system as "invisible" for students. When questions were asked about the computers, the answers were ones of surprise that anyone would ask, and they would refer to them with nonchalance. They have simply grown up in a time when everything has been high tech, and it's only the older folks (past age thirty) who seemed to be enamored by new equipment. As someone referred to us nontechnocrats, we are "digital immigrants."

We also found that computer classes were useless. When young people have the time and freedom to actually use computers as they would in real life, they teach each other very quickly and efficiently. All the students in our schools know virtually every program commonly available, and many have become programmers or graphic and animation experts and can produce brilliant, creative, and first-rate electronic productions.

At EdVisions we like the thinking of Alan November, national speaker and consultant. He says that there should be few limitations on academic computing and that every opportunity to use technology to research and demonstrate should be made available. In talking to students, they don't count on school to be the place they get their best experiences with technology, and many have more equipment at home. It's the adults who are having the hardest time adapting to the new technologies and freeing their minds up to see the possibilities. And a technology committee makes about as much sense as having a chalkboard committee a hundred years ago.

Our belief in putting teachers in charge of school operations goes against the grain of normal school operations. We know it, accept it, and understand the repercussions. It's not been easy to actually carry out or to convince teachers this is a viable and valuable option. Few young educators are confident they can run schools, and many older teachers are weary of the long hours and tenuous conditions of starting and running new schools. In Minnesota, we've been assisted by the charter law that states "a majority of the board shall be made up teachers teaching in the school" and by our teacher professional practice model. This calls for true site management, something far different from the token roles of the more familiar version seen in many school districts.

We believe teachers can and should run small schools, and the benefit of doing so far outweigh the negatives. Although many teacher–leaders come to us with interest and excitement, not all have the tools to lead a functioning school and a very different learning program. We find it most important to help prepare those who want to go forward and do as much as we can to assist them. The results of teachers leading are often no less demanding but can be very rewarding. Many describe the experience as the single most exhilarating professional experience of their lives.

As a core reason for creating the New Country School and EdVisions Cooperative, we think schools should give serious consideration to at least pursuing the idea of a governance model that challenges the notion of professionals serving at the will of an administrator. We have found a distributive leadership model, where the staff hones its expertise so that each key player becomes the expert in one or two areas, really can be a viable alternative to the distant involvement and distant accountability of top-down models.

In addition, high school students can and should have a greater say in what happens in schools as well. Student government models should be taken seriously. They not only are a great learning opportunity but also can be a valuable asset to the overall leadership of good schools.

So why do this? Why would a respectable group of educators and businesspeople put their careers on the line to spend long days and sleepless nights forging what many will never accept as mainstream schooling? The ensuing chapters will delve into the heart and soul of what drove the planners and what continues to push the teacher–leaders in the EdVisions schools. The contributing authors to this book ask these questions every day of themselves and those working in the EdVisions schools. Little did we know those coffee shop meetings would result in the hope and inspiration to help lead a movement of small, innovative high schools. Little did we know that over 500 visitors a year would walk through the door of our small school to get a glimpse of students creating their own learning. And little did we know that what we thought were just commonsense notions would mesh together to create something so powerful to be worthy of replication.

We believe the world is changing rapidly. The information age is well upon us now. It's not something coming in the future or something we should prepare for meekly. Young people are not going to sit and wait for information to be delivered to them no matter how important we adults think that information might be. Schools will have to become more interesting and more relevant, and they may not be where kids expect to get the larger share of their learning. That will shock a few people who suffer from what Ron Newell calls a "peculiar conceit." And young teachers are not going to work in places that treat them as assembly line workers. They too are products of the information age. If we've done anything in this new thinking about students, schools, and teachers, it's that it has run head-on into the future with some old-fashioned community values.

3

Student Ownership: Teacher Ownership

Ron Newell

When the Minnesota New Country School (MNCS) was born, out of a great deal of thinking, visioning, and physical labor, no one had any idea we were creating something that would gain notoriety. We did have in mind creating something we knew would work better for adolescents. Most of us who created the school had negative experiences in the traditional setting—not necessarily negative for us personally but negative in the sense that we knew there were certain structures in place that were barriers to students doing the best they could. And there were barriers to us as teachers doing what we knew worked for powerful learning.

For example, many of the educators involved with MNCS knew that projects captivated and motivated students. Yet with coverage issues, time-based courses, and a text-driven curriculum, projects became the second-class citizens of the learning community. Another method we knew worked well for learning is allowing students to have choices of what to study and what projects they could create. Another element we knew captivated and motivated students was computers and computer applications. Computers had not been incorporated into the typical classroom structure to be advantageous for student learning.

What we all knew or felt intuitively was that incorporating the three elements of choice, projects, and computers would build student ownership of their own education.

Ownership is necessary in order to enable students' self-reliance and self-efficacy and to develop lifelong learning skills. Those are the elements of learning we felt were necessary outcomes for a high school program.

Knowing this, the founding group decided to place those three powerful motivators for learning at the forefront and let other things go. We decided courses and classes would take second place to students choosing projects and students using computers. From that humble beginning, a most progressive, student-centered, integrated, project-based program was initiated.

When we began, my first reaction to all the hard work of going through the chartering process, the development of a physical site, recruiting students, talking with parents and civic groups, and so on led me to think, "Students had better show they are really eager to learn after we give them all this incentive—or else I will count it a failure." My first reaction to dealing with the students was that mouthing the words "student centered" didn't turn students on to learning. Just telling them they now could do projects they were interested in was not enough to excite them. The reasons are many: 1) they didn't know how to do long-term projects because they were not used to doing them and rarely had choices; 2) they were still in the antagonist mode in regard to relationship with teachers; and 3) after many years of frustrating experiences in their previous school settings, many of the students had some psychological pathologies to deal with.

Students after six to ten years in the traditional system are not able to think on their own; indeed, they are rewarded for regurgitating information in the "answering pedagogy," not for thinking for themselves. Consequently, the students had no background in independent thinking and formulating. They had to be walked through a process. The difficulty, at first, was that we had not developed a good process, and each adviser stumbled through developing a process that worked for him or her. Eventually, we talked and were able to determine some basic steps in developing projects.

But we still did not have adequate resources to help the students get the necessary information. Resources were at a premium. Even though we knew that "the world is the curriculum," we did not have adequate means of connecting students with the world. We relied on hand-me-downs (books donated by parents, libraries, and old school texts) and on the computer resources. But first we had to connect all the computers to a network and the Internet, and this was time consuming.

We wanted to take students out of the building to businesses, to museums, and to research facilities, to awaken, it was hoped, an interest in some real-world activity on which to base a project. When many of the field trips did not lead to meaningful projects, we knew there had to be some process whereby students could connect meaningful resources to meaningful learning opportunities. This had to be in the process of creating projects. The first necessity was to build on whatever student choice there was, even if it did not appear to have much merit in the standard school sense. When students could investigate their interests first, they then could be led to more in-depth projects that met state standards.

In all cases they were utilizing various process-oriented skills—finding resources, reading, analyzing, synthesizing, writing, organizing thoughts, and creatively demonstrating ways to show learning. When some good projects did come forth and when we had taken some meaningful field trips, when advisers could connect those projects with the state standards, then students began to see purpose in the project-based approach. This, however, took time to develop and did not immediately occur.

Also, when given choice, relationships with students became better because the old antagonisms began to disintegrate. Most adolescents and preadolescents have experienced enough school time to see school as an antagonistic place, a place where adults tell you what to do and when to do it. Consequently, adolescents balk at doing what they are told and will try to do something contrary. It was very difficult for many of the first-year students to connect with the accountability piece—that, indeed, they were the ones who were responsible for their own learning. Many students still used age-old excuses for not getting started or finishing with projects—the "dog ate my homework" kinds of excuses. When students began to realize that their advisers could not offer credit until projects that met standards were completed and that mere "seat time" was not adequate, most discarded that mode of thinking and began to see the advisers as protagonists rather than antagonists.

This was one of the most difficult transitions of all. Students had to see that use of their time toward purposeful action—that is, creating and producing products that showed their acquisition of knowledge or skills—was critical. Credit could not be earned by just being there, acting cute, or ig-noring the advisers.

Part of making that a reality for students was creating a checklist and documentation of time applied to learning activities. Another element was asking students to journal about their learning experiences. When students began to acknowledge how serious those activities were, use of time be-came more purposeful, and that resulted in better projects.

Some of the advisers felt that the students needed immediate gratifi-cation for their work. One of the results of that was the development of validating a small number of projects (book reports, short essays, re-search projects of little depth, and so on) that provided immediate feed-back rather than encouraging deeper, longer-term research projects. Stu-dents and parents were more familiar with having smaller assignments akin to traditional homework-like activities and instant gratification and were impatient waiting for long-term benefits that long-range projects were able to provide. Consequently, MNCS advisers began giving "val-idations" for these smaller projects and lost sight of the vision and mis-sion of creating lifelong learning skills. It took many months of negoti-ations and discussions between faculty and parents to return to the original plan.

Students fought this fight as well. They were more interested in being told to do some small assignments rather than plan a long-range, inte-grated project. This "pulling back" to old ways of doing things was dis-appointing to some of us, perhaps comforting to others on staff. When you are creating something new from a larger vision, it is easy to lose your way. Thankfully, over the first three years, staff members came on board who fought for the progressive, student interest–driven project model. Not until a good proposal format and checklists were created did students feel more comfortable.

As mentioned earlier, there would be a great deal of disappointment if students did not feel empowered and take a great interest in learning from this process. There were disappointments because there were students who did not show an interest in anything that looked like "work" in the school sense. Some adapted to the process very early and did extremely well. There were a number of students who did not use time well, who continually fought the system, and who still played the old games. Some of those students simply had to find their way and learn that they could be self-motivated and self-reliant. With patience on part of the parents and teachers, project-based learning began to become a reality.

Creating caring relationships between advisers and students generally caused a turnaround in many of the students who balked at doing the work. The relationships between adviser and student and student to student were central to creating a culture of caring. When a culture of caring became real, most students responded by becoming responsible for their own education. When the atmosphere was no longer one of antagonism, when students saw that they were empowered, they usually did well. The first years of MNCS are full of examples of students who accomplished little initially, sometimes for many months, but then made rapid progress, accomplished great projects, and met standards enough to catch up to their peers.

Many adolescents do not learn on the same time line as expected in time-based, curriculum-based schools. They have stops and starts and fits of creative and almost manic accomplishment and often have times of reflective pondering. Asking all of them to accomplish the same amount of work on the same assignments over the period of semesters or years is apt to cause some to fail. Asking the students to accomplish standards and skills in order to graduate *on their own time* proved eventually to motivate a greater number of students. But not all. Some still languished, and the parents panicked, thinking they needed to show progress in the same manner as in traditional settings. Some did not develop the self-discipline needed to be self-directed.

So, the question was asked, "Is this a type of school for everyone?" The answer appeared to be, "No, it was not." Who, then, is it for, and who is it not for? Ten years later that is still difficult to answer. Each person has his or her own reason for coming to a project-based, student interest–driven school. But by interviews with students who came to these environments, some conclusions can be drawn.

First, many left their old high schools because of feelings of nonacceptance. Cliques, gangs, bullies, and peer pressure asked the young people to conform and be something they were not. Or they were kept in "their place" by teasing and bullying. Getting into a small-school atmosphere and into advisory groups of multiaged adolescents and preadolescents allowed for students to be well known and accepted for themselves. When observing any one of the sites utilizing the advisory group and project-based model, one sees very little negative peer pressure. Smallness and family-style structures can alleviate much of the pain of the maturing process. This smallness and family-like atmosphere are not often associated with traditional larger schools.

Second, many reported feeling bored with school in the traditional setting. That boredom came from having to do similar things in every class and from redundant coverage of the same material. Or it sometimes was due to lack of challenge for those who could readily grasp core content. Another aspect of this boredom was the lack of interesting activities in classes. Just sitting and taking notes and regurgitating for tests made middle and high school very difficult for many.

The project-based model allows student choice rather than teacher choice of curriculum, and learning is not time-based. This allows for a less boring atmosphere and challenges the adolescent mind. Interest-driven projects and choice allow for the brain to be engaged, which increases motivation and attention. This in turn triggers actual changes in brain chemistry, with the brain producing endorphins, chemicals that allow for attitudes of "I can" and "I will."

The positive changes that occurred led to a powerful attitude of ownership on the part of students. Giving them choice of content and when to study proved to be a catalyst for a great deal of other changes in students' perception of school. Creating individual workstations for students proved to be another catalytic event. This was a huge change for high school students to be able to walk into a building and find they have a space that is their very own. It allowed them to think of the building as theirs and not belonging to teachers or a principal. Removing them from the classroom mentality required such a change, and it was a momentous decision on the part of the founders to allow for this change in structure.

At first it appeared as if the concept would backfire, as students did nothing but decorate their space with typical teenage stuff—pictures of rock stars, athletes, movie stars, and so on. It became necessary to monitor student areas for a variety of possible "moral outrages," and eventually rules had to be clarified as to what "personal" meant in a public setting. It was a good lesson, though, and eventually the silliness over it lessened, and the workstation became just that—a workspace. Today at MNCS and at replica sites, a visitor would find nothing more unusual than what exists in typical office spaces.

Allowing for students to make choices in how they used their day became the largest hurdle (along with creating projects that met standards), as students had difficulty planning purposeful time. It was difficult for advisers to keep students on track, and eventually many time management–oriented rubrics were devised, along with project credits with the number of hours utilized being part of the assessment. When the students observed the value attached by the advisers to the documentation of time, eventually they became more purposeful.

Many positive results occurred for students because of the allowance of choice in performance-based, active, authentic learning (see the longitudinal study done by Hamline University, chapter 9). Choice, coupled with teachers who cared, made for a powerful dynamic that was synthesized into an innovative and unique learning environment. As we anticipated, ownership for their work and for their own education was the eventual outcome.

The teachers exercised their choice when they decided to leave the traditional system to create this innovative school. We also exercised a great deal of choice when we made judgments regarding the type of school that would be created: the appearance of the building, the type of technology and how it would be used, the curriculum that students needed to accomplish, the students' voice in decision making, and how we would govern the school. Because the Minnesota charter law created teacher majority school boards, teachers automatically became owners of the enterprise.

Ownership, however, is the result when teachers exercise their decision-making powers in making daily choices regarding the manner in which they are to educate the students under their care. In the traditional setting, teachers make hundreds or thousands of decisions each day, but those decisions are typically much different than for those who operate charter schools. Every day we had to make decisions relative to dealing with each student personally, what resources to use for each, what amount of time we could afford individuals and groups, how to guide students rather than give them information, what policies were needed to give the school the proper atmosphere for learning, how to deal with computers and Internet information, how to spend the public money, and how to respond to the state's many bureaucratic needs.

The difference in this decision making versus the traditional was huge—how to operate the whole school, how to market and keep parents happy, how to involve the community in projects and students in community service, and so on. Consequently, ownership was more palpable than merely having control over what happened in one's classroom.

Eventually the small staff had to figure out how to budget and keep the finances in line with state guidelines, how to report student information to the state, and all the other "stuff" that was required of charters. Who said charters were exempt from rules and regulations? The exemptions were so very few that they barely registered. The small staff of four was eventually overwhelmed by all the paperwork.

The founders also created a teacher-owned cooperative as a support system for the school. A radically different concept, the cooperative idea was developed out of two basic needs: to show that teachers could organize in a different way other than to be under a union contract with a district school board and to give an entrepreneurial and collegial sense of ownership as an organization. The cooperative allowed for another level of ownership. The cooperative contracted for payroll and benefits, not the school. As the co-op became larger, this made sense in saving money on insurance and benefits packages. The cooperative was eventually able to hire a person to accomplish the bookwork and administrative work to allow for the teachers to deal with program issues. Once the school was more viable and had program procedures in place, they were able to hire personnel from within who could complete the work, paying stipends to teachers who did administrative work in addition to regular duties.

The co-op also allowed the opportunity for outreach by obtaining grants and utilizing co-op personnel to develop and operate new charters. It appeared to be a pipe dream at first, but time proved that it could and did happen. Various grants were obtained through a nonprofit created by the co-op, and the association gained extra work for co-op members.

When a co-op member became involved in the co-op and worked with other sites in operations, ownership in the bigger picture became a reality. The association made available workshops, provided personnel for consultation, and developed handbooks and guidebooks for new charters to follow so they would not have to "reinvent the wheel." The guidebook provided procedural processes and a process for doing staff evaluation.

The development of staff evaluation, budgeting, merit pay scales, and ideals contributed to a sense of ownership. Every member who worked in a school had to go through a process of review and evaluation. Consequently, everyone realized they were part of an enterprise that necessitated developing themselves as well-prepared professionals who had positive effects on students. If they did not take that to heart, they would soon find that keeping a viable and popular school for students and parents as their educational home would be difficult.

Operating a charter school and making daily decisions that affected the whole enterprise most assuredly led to a sense of ownership. But simply having a dream that was realized, seeing students coming to school happy when they previously were truant, seeing and hearing parents talk about how happy their children were to come to the school, and seeing the meaningful projects that students presented to the public gave the founders a greater sense of ownership than anything else. Maybe every teacher dreams of developing and running his or her own school. There would be a great deal of satisfaction and feeling of ownership if one was created, it become a reality, and it became popular enough that others adopted the model.

It is the same sense of ownership a student must feel when they accomplish the whole curriculum, meet all the project credits needed, and create products that are unique and creative. "I did it. I can do more. I will accomplish what I set out to accomplish." This is the kind of ownership that creates self-efficacy and confidence. Teachers who create and operate their own schools feel that same sense of self-efficacy and ownership and can be proud of what they accomplish.

4

The EdVisions Project Approach: Facilitating Student Choice

Ron Newell

There is much research in education that has come to light the past ten years pertaining to how young people learn best. For example, the November 2002 edition of *Educational Leadership* magazine included a number of articles on best practices. These are some of the paraphrased statements from the authors of those articles:

> Invite kids to learn; move and inspire them; accept learners as persons; learners must contribute and make a difference; learners must have purpose; learners must have the power to choose; learners need to be challenged, have accountability.
>
> —Tomlinson

> Student engagement is gauged by "flow"—doing what is considered both work and play. Flow comes from: extracurricular activities, computer use, group work, individual tasks, relevance, creativity, discovering what you do well, having support for the activity. Reflection helps flow.
>
> —Csikszentmilhalyi

> Utilize local problem-solving through place-based learning. Solve real problems; activate desire to learn through interests.
>
> —Smith

Create a climate of caring. Have discourse with open-ended questions. Learners will accept responsibility for their own behaviors if they own their own ideas.

—Roberts

Projects have power if topics are based upon the learner's interests as well as the curriculum and standards. Arrange opportunities for students to do field work. Have a culminating event, such as presentations of student work.

—Curtis

Allow student choice; integrate the curriculum; differentiate (personalize) learning; cultivate self-assessment.

—Brown

Allow students to construct their own learning opportunities; use multiple connections to integrate subjects; allow student voice.

—Findley

Students want responsibility; personalize learning; show caring; promote active, experiential learning; maintain high expectations; allow self-directed learning; allow student opinion.

—Easton

Renate and Geoffrey Caine (1997) also have written extensively on brain learning principles. They identified three principles—creating a state of "relaxed alertness," curriculum and activities ought to be built around "orchestrated immersion," and "active processing" (38) ought to be realized whenever possible. With those principles in place, a school would have individualized learning plans for all learners, integrate the curriculum, and create processes for project-based learning. Students would learn not only facts but also how to access them and how to use them. There would be increased motivation due to having choice. Higher-order thinking skills would be stressed as opposed to learning only facts. And a real-world audience would be available to witness and judge student work.

The previous statements give a taste of what educational experience and research has been saying about project-based learning for years. We as educators have known for a long time that these things are true. The problem has been that very few schools have attempted project-based learning because it does not fit into the traditional daily structure of school—a day that is course based, time based, curriculum based, and established for control of masses of children. As powerful as project-based learning is, you will find that it is used sparingly and usually as an element of regular classes or as a special program. Consequently, opportunity for effective learning experiences is reduced.

At the Minnesota New Country School, students have to formulate projects from their own interests and apply them to state standards. In the process they also have to apply time and effort into meeting quality standards in order to achieve the required number of project credits to graduate. The project-based system at the New Country School is built around student choice of topic, thereby being student interest driven. Why give students choice of projects? Choice is one of the most powerful inducers of enthusiasm and curiosity.

When people are given choice, the limbic system and frontal lobes are engaged, creating conditions that are optimal for thinking. As Tomlinson says in his article in *Educational Leadership*, invite kids to learn, move and inspire them; learners must have the power to choose.

How can a school function effectively when adolescents are given choices of what to study? The choice factor builds interest in learning and "opens the door" to other engagements and other learning styles. But if left to their devices, adolescents do not consistently make altogether wise decisions about what to learn, when to learn, and how to learn. Therefore, educators and staff of the New Country School over the years developed a daily structure and a process for implementing student interest–driven projects. The process helped students make better use of their time, track activities, do reflection activities, and embed state standards while in the process of learning about their interests. This is the "orchestrated immersion" part of brain-based learning.

Many questions are asked about pure student-driven, project-based learning. Does it help students learn factual information? Do these students do well on standardized tests? Are they accepted into college? The answer is yes to all the above. First and foremost, you cannot complete a project without factual information. And if you start with state standards as the lead into information and the final judge of whether the correct information is embedded, then the factual information necessary to meet state standards is not only present but also utilized in such a manner as to give meaning. Second, because the information has context, it is more memorable to the student than information read or given in a time-based curriculum and used only to pass a test.

Why was a project-based system devised? The previous quotes and paraphrases of research and example give the reader the best response. It was a powerful learning practice in the experience of professionals who attempted to use the process. The design team of the New Country School realized that time-based courses, fragmented curriculum, management, and control factors only stood in the way of powerful learning opportunities and did not facilitate them. It was necessary to devise a more interesting and relevant way for young adults to learn and to be connected to the real world. The best educational environments create conditions for challenging and connected learning. It is much more challenging to identify a problem or question and design a plan based on a real project than to read a chapter and answer the questions.

When engaging learners in comprehensive projects, students learn not only process skills but content as well. Reading and writing skills automatically improve, as do acquiring, analyzing, and synthesizing information. The process drives the learning of factual information, and, in addition, the information is used for a real purpose. Teachers who have experienced long-term projects know that students learn factual information even better when doing projects than when attending to regular course work. The only difference is that the information retained is not always neatly organized into curricular bundles. Therefore, students may not show the same factual learning at the same time as others who have done a course-based and graded curriculum.

Project-based learning connects students to the real world. This, coupled with choice, makes the learning activity relevant, engaging, and challenging. This brings about the condition of "flow" as mentioned in the article in *Educational Leadership* by Csikszentmilhalyi mentioned previously, a condition that appears to be both work and play at the same time. It is apparent to any visitor of the New Country School that students are engaged and purposeful (although not necessarily quiet). Place-based learning, service learning, and community involvement allow for authentic learning experiences that build real-life skills such as time management, teamwork, communication, planning, self-assessment, and adjustment. Students learn real problem solving, not artificial and/or hypothetical problem solving.

This authenticity and use of choice creates conditions for the development of intrinsic motivation rather than the constant use of extrinsic motivation often utilized in traditional high schools. Classroom management has become a science, with many texts and college courses based on creating conditions for grouped adolescents to learn the same thing simultaneously. Threats, inducements, rewards, grades, graduation, and the spite of parents, teachers, and society at large appear to be the prime motivating factors. Rewards may seem positive, but there is research showing that even rewards create an artificial learning that is temporary. When there is intrinsic motivation, there is a heightened sense of alertness, enthusiasm, and interest in accepting challenges.

Customizing the learning for each student allows for the learning environment and tasks to be tailored to each person's strengths and learning styles. It also allows for the tailoring of the learning activity to the person's weaknesses and needs. If a student needs specific improvement in reading skills, writing skills, math skills, and so on, it is possible to create projects that meet the student's needs. Students fairly quickly come to understand that good reading and writing skills are needed in order to present their work in public presentations. Math skills are more difficult to identify as a need, but if for no other reason, the ability to meet basic skill levels to pass statewide tests will be a motivator. In some situations, math skills will be needed in an authentic project (such as demographic statistics), and the student will acknowledge the need for understanding various math skills.

Customizing for the individual needs is akin to the adviser/teacher acting as a general practice M.D.: apply diagnostic procedures, identify the ailment by observing the symptoms, and acknowledging that you are not qualified to remedy the situation, you seek a qualified expert. If a student needs better reading or math skills than a generalist teacher can provide, he or she finds an expert, either on staff or elsewhere, who will design a program for the learning of those skills. This, then, becomes the project for that learner (see the senior project about learning to read in chapter 2).

The same can be said for the high achiever or gifted student who can complete projects on a wide variety of choices with greater ease. Perhaps their concern is for obtaining a good ACT score. They may make a project out of studying for the math portion of the test (for example, by utilizing over-the-counter aids). The adviser facilitates according to the learner's needs. The structure of the school was based on personalizing the education of every student, with every student having an individualized learning plan.

Perhaps the question arises, What kind of structure allows for project-based learning to take place? A structure of daily practice that includes a process leading the student from brainstorming to collecting resources to embedding standards to developing products to being assessed. The project proposal process developed by the New Country School, the checklists and the rubrics for identifying effective learning, have been developed and are utilized by students and staff every day.

A second thing necessary to facilitate project-based learning is a set of standards that are available to students and understood by staff and students (and parents as well). The staff at the New Country School recognized initially that the students would have to know what learning goals were expected of them. Standards were written in booklet form and made available to each student. There were no secrets. It was the desire of the staff to ensure that students understood the factual information and process skills expected by the state. Then interests could be tailored toward those standards. The thinking was (and is) that whatever interest a student investigates would also involve some of the discipline standards in some manner or form.

For example, everything requires reading, analyzing, and synthesizing in some medium of communication. So communication skills were being "validated" with practically every project. If the project was about horses, then biology, geography, history, economics, and so on could be included in the project proposal. This process helped students become aware of the breadth and depth of topics and helped them to broaden their perspectives on their interests. And the process enabled students to eventually understand that school is about learning a body of knowledge and skills rather than an exercise in "putting in your time" as school appears to be too often.

A third reason for adopting the pure project-based system is the adviser–advisee system. Instead of being a "homeroom," advisories at the New Country School are actual advisory groups that are formed into "learning circles." A student is assigned or chooses an adviser, and that adviser becomes their mentor, guide, facilitator, assessor, teacher, and advocate throughout the project processes undertaken by that student. An adviser has that student and possibly sixteen or seventeen more students in the group. The advisory, always located in the same area of the building, meets twice every day, undertakes group activities, and is led by the same adviser. The adviser is expected to monitor their seventeen or eighteen advisees' project credits, life skills, and standards. This allows them to have the time to interact with other students (to provide them with areas of expertise other advisers may not have) and to undertake the chores necessary to keep the school operating.

There is a means by which students can choose their advisers (after the initial arrival at the school) so that choice and interests and personalities can be respected and complemented for optimum success. If an adviser–advisee relationship is not working, then the student can be switched to another adviser. Students have a choice of their top three advisers for the following year, and barring overloading any one adviser, each usually gets their first or second choice. Students can stay with the same adviser for the entire six years of matriculation. The system allows for the development of meaningful and supporting relationships, advisers developing greater knowledge of their students, and students becoming better acquainted with a significant adult other than a parent.

A fourth element that is needed to implement the pure project-based system is creating a means by which every student can have his or her own workstation. The advisories are organized so that there are spaces for seventeen to twenty workstations in the same open area of a building. Students may organize and use their station as they wish so that there is a total ownership by the student of that space. The allowance for individual spaces has empowered students and advisers, who have their desks in strategic space within the advisory, to operate as individuals.

Personalizing the building gave the message that each student was an important person and that the school was about individual work, not classroom work. It also showed students they were trusted. Students most often have a computer at their station, can use headphones, have snacks, use organizers to keep resource materials handy, and so on. The students feel at home and therefore see the whole school as an extension of *their* lives instead of some brick-and-mortar edifice not of their choosing. It is their school and does not belong to the adults who work in the building.

This personalization is accompanied with the fifth element: flexible access to and use of the building. Staff at the New Country School has found that having a large open space with tables and chairs that allows for flexible use and for large-group presentations is much more valuable than a group of classrooms. It is recommended that each building have breakout rooms, an art space, a shop, a science area where experiments can be facilitated, and so on but no rows of classroom that "belong" to a teacher. This flexibility allows for presentations of student work and for groups and individuals to display their handiwork, provides a meeting place for organizing group projects, enables math groups to work together, and provides for an all-school meeting. Trying to accommodate pure project-based learning in a traditional building is difficult and ought to be avoided if possible.

By this time, the reader has recognized that accomplishing project-based learning to its fullest extent means that school cannot be school as usual. No courses, no bells, no blackboards, no teachers in front of a class lecturing, no unit tests, no movement of large groups through the halls— and no stampede of students out the door when the last bell rings. Rather the opposite: students don't want to leave the building. One of the most interesting phenomena we found in that first year was that many students stayed well after the time designated, working on the computer or finishing up some aspect of a product.

The system devised by the founders and practitioners of the New Country School developed a project-based learning system that dispensed with all the old ideas about education systems. Adolescents can be trusted to be self-motivated and responsible if given a choice in their own education. Students care when they have been cared for and nurtured. When not forced by a time-based, curriculum-based, and teacher-constructed system to be a passive recipient of adult-driven activities, adolescent students respond with adult-like behavior. When supported by caring, nurturing, knowledgeable generalist practitioners, adolescent students will be responsible and purposeful. The project-based system devised by the Minnesota New Country School works well in guiding young people toward participating in life as purposeful adults.

REFERENCE

Caine, R., & Caine, G. (1997). *Education on the edge of possibility.* Alexandria, VA: Association for Supervision and Curriculum Development.

Part 2

BUILDING THE LEARNING COMMUNITY

The following four essays were written by critical friends of EdVisions and the Minnesota New Country School. All these persons have influenced the replication and creation of the great small learning communities in the EdVisions network and continue to influence the work of changing everything!

5

Building a Learning Community:
The Conscious Pursuit of an Idea

Walter Enloe

Little did I know thirty years ago that I would be helping educators create and sustain small learning communities, contributing to a rapidly growing cultural transformation in formal schooling in the United States. This revolution is not a recent concept. Personally, I define it in terms of basic ideas about human nature: part–whole, passive–active, evil–good, nature–nurture, individual–society, unilateral respect–mutual respect, and authority–autonomy, among others. Perhaps Jean Piaget, the most eminent researcher of human development and an early proponent of active learning and democratic pedagogy (*l'ecole active*), captures best my thinking over the years. He wrote this explanation of human rights and education ("activity versus passivity") following his "The Right to Education in the Present World" in honor of the Universal Declaration of Human Rights:

> The principal goal of education is to create people who are capable of doing new things, not simply repeating what other generations have done — people who are creators, inventors, discoverers. The second goal of education is to form minds that are critical, can verify, and do not accept everything they are offered. The great danger today is from slogans, collective opinions, ready-made trends of thought. We have to be able to resist individually, to criticize, and to distinguish between what is proven and what is not. So we need pupils who are active, who learn early to find out for themselves, partly by their own spontaneous activity and partly through the

materials we set up for them; who learn early to tell what is verifiable and what is simply the first idea to come to them.

At EdVisions, not only do we respect and mutually learn from our colleagues and contemporaries, but we also honor each other's personal and collective history. The fundamental principles that we espouse—teacher and student ownership of their (our) lives and work—has developmental and historical antecedents and origins. Roland Barth's *Learning by Heart* (2001) captures the essence of our work together at EdVisions: "The way to learn is by leading; the way to lead is by learning. Teacher leadership provides an inevitable and continual occasion for teacher growth. The teacher who is always leading and learning will generate students who are capable of both leading and learning."

My initiation to the profession began in 1991 as a graduate student at Emory's Graduate Institute of Liberal Arts, where I found a first-year learning community at the Paideia School. I began as an aide in the half-day two-and-a-half- to five-year-old program. Over the next eight years, I was learning and teaching in the K–12 multiage, multigrade groupings, where I developed my interests in human development, social justice, and learning in community. I became an assistant and coteacher for four years before I became a lead teacher of the half-day kindergarten. I later became an adviser in the high school, learning from master leaders and learners and teachers, honored in such texts as *Creating Context* (Enloe 1996) and Collay et al.'s *Learning Circles: Creating Conditions for Professional Development* (1998).

While at Paideia, three books were to determine my future lifework: Herb Kohl's *The Open Classroom* (1969), which led me to the understanding that open is not lack of structure but a complex, living system; Roland Barth's *Open Education and the American School* (1972), which gave me the idea of "living learning"; and Howard Gardner's *The Quest for Mind: Piaget, Levi-Strauss and the Structuralist Movement* (1973), which led me to see Piaget's lifework as an "open system."

I came to Minnesota in 1988 to codirect the rural and Minnesota component of the National Models School Project in Global Education. The project was led by the American Forum in New York and based on the work of John Goodlad (school reform) and Kenneth Boulding (systems theory). The project asked school communities to determine through community forums and school committees what values, attitudes, skills, and knowledge students needed to live productive lives in the twenty-first century and what practices, organizations, and programs schools needed for students to acquire such values. While that project was important and helped instill an international and global perspective into some schools' curriculum, it was my earlier experiences at the Paideia School in Atlanta and then at the International School in Hiroshima that best inform my consultations and "critical friend" role with EdVisions schools. Little did we know then that today, at the dawn of the new millennia and new century, my earlier work would come together in helping to create great, small schools.

My experience at Paideia helped impact how I, as a teacher–principal, lead Hiroshima International School from 1980 to 1988 in the organization, curriculum, and philosophy we established there. Paideia has continued to develop from its inception in 1970 to become "a school of national character." It began as a small school of a 150 K–6 students. We deliberately grew the student body in the nine years I was there to 450 K–12 students (today it has around 950 and still feels and thinks small).

Years later, in 1982, Mortimer Adler and associates created the Paideia school model (*The Paideia Proposal*, 1982). I've never been able to establish a direct or correlative link between the original Paideia school and the Paideia school movement. There are similarities in philosophy and practice, but there are several key distinctions. First is the definition of the Greek term *paideia*. For the original school, the definition was and continues to be "the conscious pursuit of a series of educational goals by a community. It conveys the concept of a child's total education: intellectual, artistic, and social." For the Adler group, today organized as Paideia Group Inc. (http://www. paideiapgi), *paideia* means "the upbringing of a child."

I am frequently asked to identify a model of a world-class school, and the Paideia School in Atlanta comes to mind (I can no longer speak for Hiroshima International School, though I know it is an excellent small school). For example, when Avalon Charter School of St. Paul, an EdVisions School, constituted itself as a learning community with professional ownership and a project and seminar approach, the question was asked, Shouldn't the students also govern themselves; or better, shouldn't the whole community be involved?

That insight led us back to the Paideia Middle School. Over thirty years ago, Bernie and Martha Schein and their colleagues created and sustained a student congress and constitution. Being good students of human culture, we borrowed and refined their model. When Chris Hazelton of Harbor City International School in Duluth, Minnesota (another EdVisions School), asked me in the early school planning where he could find a place where the members of the school lived out their values, I invited him to immerse himself in the lifeworld of the Paideia School in Atlanta. I suggested he begin in the lifeworld of a five-year-old because it was a good beginning place to feel and think deeply about high school learners and suitable environments. And when Larry Rosenstock consulted with me about creating Big River Montessori High School, which has a sacred balance between content and process, between historical achievement and human novelty, I encouraged him, once again, to visit Paideia. I'm reminded of a number of recollections that might capture why I still hold so dear this model of developing and sustaining a learning community.

In 1979–1980, I cochaired the Paideia Self-Study. After investigating whether to join the Southern Association of Schools and College, which seemed more interested in quantity and the number of toilets we had than in quality and the kinds of learning and teaching we promoted, we decided to do our own investigation. We asked retired Emory University educator Newt Hodgson to be a "critical friend." When you go to the school's current website (http://www.paideiaschool.org), the first thing you find is a Hodgson quote from that self-study:

> Above all else, a good school should be a good place for people to be. It should exemplify qualities of human interaction that we would wish for people everywhere. One should feel valued. A great many interesting things should be going on. One should be learning a lot—especially learning how better to learn. School should be a place one looks forward to going to in the morning and somewhat reluctant to end at the end of the day. The school as a center for learning should have things going on in the evenings and on weekends involving parents and people from the surrounding community as well as students and faculty.

The next year (1980), I went to Hiroshima International School (HIS) as a teacher–principal, where I remained until 1988. I rewrote the school's brochure, borrowing the precise language from Paideia to convey our mission:

HIS's philosophy is based on the belief that schools can be informal and individualized, yet still educate well. We believe that a quality education acknowledges the innate curiosity of children and their desire to understand and master their environment. Because children have different interests and learning styles, and because they progress at different rates, we take considerable care to tailor our program to the talents and needs of each learner. We think our concern for intellectual achievement and discipline is compatible with personal consideration of the needs of each child and with an informal school environment.

A final insight: Paideia has continued to develop a learning community for thirty-five years by refining its essential principles rather than following a prescribed ideology. Actions speak louder than words alone rarely do. We believe that every school is a complex social community with the assigned task of passing on to the younger generation some of the knowledge and skill acquired by the older generation. It is fundamental to us that we examine what we are teaching in addition to academic knowledge: how we view the larger human community, how we treat each other as individuals, how we relate to the physical environment, how we view the process and content of learning. We need to examine what we teach as part of the way we live and interact with each other as a community of adults and children. The Paideia School and EdVisions Schools presume that families choose their school community in part because they perceive that the school shares many of their values. Following is a quote from Paideia today:

> While the primary teaching of values belongs to the family, the school is in the unique position of being able to mediate between a more impersonal social order and the intensely personal family experience. It is the school's responsibility to help prepare children for a place in the society; we also hope that the school environment can have some of the personal depth and meaningfulness of family life. We hope that our students will be prepared not only to live in the world but to improve it. These principles already exist at Paideia, and they will continue to be expressed in the life of the school. We list them because we recognize the importance of saying out loud what we treasure:
>
> 1. excellence and hard work
> 2. attitudes toward learning

3. respect for diversity
4. social responsibility
5. egalitarianism
6. empathy
7. development of an ethical self
8. commitment to an environmental view
9. an appreciation of the importance of the present

When Paideia opened in 1971, its nucleus of teachers were young and had studied at Harvard's School of Education, which was promoting "informal" or "open" education from Great Britain. (Charles Rathbone once told me that he and Roland Barth at Harvard coined that term in the mid-1960s.) Several of us had studied the "new education" at innovative Eckerd College, among others. While Piaget was essential for helping us understand developing children and their need for a collaborative, creative, constructive learning environment, it was Barth's *Open Education and the American School* (1972), Kohl's *The Open Classroom* (1969), and Piaget's seminal essay "The Genesis of the New Methods" (1936) that became my most valuable resources on learning and teaching.

Another seminal text was *The Long Haul: An Autobiography* (1989), cowritten by Herb Kohl (who later taught at Hamline University) and Judith Kohl and written by Myles Horton. (It was Joe Nathan who had first introduced the Kohls to Horton and the Highlander Folk Center.) In the book, Herb Kohl shared the struggles in his first year of teaching the great lessons he learned about learning cultures, developing people, and self-understanding and learning at an "open environment and with an "open attitude," which he explained is quite different from a "permissive" attitude and "permissive" environment.

Both Barth and Kohl are recommended reading by anyone beginning a new learning community. Barth's book was based on his dissertation at Harvard, written at the same time members of the original Paideia faculty were studying there. It was a case study of seven teachers (he was a teacher–principal) trying to create a new school based on "open education" principles Barth had learned from his study of informal elementary education in Leicestershire, England.

In 1975, while teaching half-day kindergarten, I remember vividly the evening I was responsible for faculty development. I typed up and distributed "Assumptions about Learning, Knowledge, and Teaching," which consisted of five pages of quotations from Barth's book and Piaget's new methods essay. Many people were fascinated by Barth's insights into learning and teaching, but as a group they were equally wary of aligning themselves to any particular program or ideology. This was not so much in reaction to the growing and vocal "back to basics" political movement as it was the inherent suspicion of any one best way to do things or the notion that one teacher "expert" or university professor had figured it all out. Instead, the school honors creativity as much as not having the right answer. It honors effort and hard work as much as accomplishment and excellence. And we honor Eleanor Duckworth's idea of the "virtue of not knowing" and, perhaps more than anything else, Goethe's notion that "in the beginning was the deed," not rhetoric.

Deliberatively building and sustaining new communities of learning can be an exciting journey in school leadership and in evolving democracy. With expectation, excitement, and risk, EdVisions schools demand that you collaborate and lead together. Though the tasks of initiating and sustaining a school are often daunting, the successes may be exhilarating and uplifting. I've had the opportunity to be involved in a number of learning communities over the past thirty-five years that not only embody the EdVisions values regarding student and teacher ownership but also demonstrate explicitly student project learning and teacher governance, both examples of people owning and being accountable for their work.

Several years ago, I sent out a postcard in the Twin Cities announcing the creation of several new public charter schools modeled on Minnesota New Country School (MNCS). It read in part, "What if teachers could design the ideal school? We can!" I received over 300 inquiries within a week. The response showed that people either were excited by an opportunity "to really create something new," the possibility of having authentic "teacher ownership," or were intrigued by the call for "passionate, inspired, and hardworking individuals to build imaginative, creative, and disciplined learning communities."

Years ago, as an "at-risk" student, I chose an experimental college, Eckerd College, which followed the traditions of diverse institutions as St. Johns, Black Mountain College, and Antioch. I continue to ask what did they mean by "at risk"—uneven test scores, the four high schools in four years, three in another country, the mixed grades? My report card from tenth grade noted "high potential, though seldom actualized."

Four years later, I graduated from an honors program where I created my own course of study, where I was president of my student government and the recipient of numerous academic and service awards. Seventeen years ago, I moved to Minnesota and was invited to offer a series of dialogues with preservice teacher candidates at a select private college down the road from MNCS. After one such facilitation, I was greeted by a professor who began his teaching career at Canadian Academy in Kobe, Japan, and was my tenth-grade history teacher. He commented, "We faculty didn't believe you would finish high school much less earn a Ph.D." I thought later, "Oh ye of little faith. How little do you realize I succeeded in spite, to spite, and despite the teachers who did not understand me as a learner much less as a whole person."

For even in such a small community of less than 150 high school students and teachers, smallness did not guarantee either personal or collective fulfillment or accomplishment. Their teaching was largely through one modality—the language of lecture. Even today, many of our best teachers refer to their work as "covering the material" or "getting through the text." I knew from the "hidden curriculum" that being a good student and a good learner meant that I was to assimilate actively in my head, but passively in my seat, as we proceeded through texts from cover to cover regurgitating correct (or incorrect) responses to end-of-chapter tests.

What I do know is that as a member of various sports teams and as an international Boy Scout during those same seldom-actualized-in-school years, I succeeded at the highest levels of performance both as a learner (twenty-one merit badges for Eagle Scout, each a separate in-depth learning project) and as a leader (camp counselor for two summers at Far East Scout Jamboree, "teaching" by demonstration and certifying scouts for the cooking and hiking merit badges).

Two great lessons I learned at Eckerd College were the ideas of student ownership and academic project work—that the learner does the learning and that if the learning institution respects the whole person, honors the learner as responsible for his learning and holds him accountable, rewards effort as well as accomplishment, and provides opportunities and mentors for actively engaging the world, the student indeed will learn. Eckerd's core book program, independent studies, and the original January term (where you studied one topic for a month) still are exemplary innovations in higher education. Those January terms, where I built a harpsichord and studied the physics of sound, studied the work of John Berryman and wrote poetry, created a one-act play, and took a lead role in a children's play, are projects that remain with me to this day.

At the International School in Hiroshima, we continued to develop an understanding through praxis of shared leadership and decision making as well as project learning. The majority of the teachers, Australian, British, and Japanese, came from "new education" traditions, which teacher David Miller often defined as "conventional book learning meets hands-on creation, exploration, and invention." Our classrooms, multiage and multinational, completed skill and concept development curriculum in the mornings with "topic" or interdisciplinary project work in the afternoons in which the concepts and skills were utilized.

The students' worldwide 1000 Cranes Club (whose stories are told in Enloe's *Lessons from Ground Zero: A Hiroshima and Nagasaki Story* [2002] and *Nagasaki Spirits, Hiroshima Voices* [2003]) is an exemplary model of student ownership, leadership, and project-based learning. Both of these books advocate embracing a current, fledgling worldwide peace movement. Based on the appeal of every living Nobel Peace Prize laureate, the United Nations General Assembly declared the decade 2001–2010 as a "Decade to Create a Culture of Peace and Nonviolence for the Children of the World," asking that all nations and communities teach peacemaking, conflict resolution, and nonviolence in their schools, neighborhoods, and workplaces. This experience helped me immeasurably in my work with current reform efforts such as EdVisions schools.

As director of the Minnesota rural component of the National Models School Project in Global Education, I worked for four years with three small districts to first determine what attitudes, skills, and knowledge community and school stakeholders believed students needed to live successfully in the twenty-first century. They then determined the best practices, programs, and learning organizations for enacting such values. It was during those years that I met leaders in the school change movement, including Doug Thomas, Dee Grover, and Joe Nathan, all of whom were to play a substantial role in the founding of MNCS.

Following the completion of that project, I had the opportunity to join a group of teachers and parents in creating the Downtown Open School in Minneapolis, a multiage, multigrade classroom school based on principles and values shared with Paideia and Hiroshima. Through the dedication and exemplary leadership of teacher Kristin Sonquist, Downtown Open became one of the pilot schools. Ernest Boyer, from the Carnegie Foundation for the Advancement of Teaching, invited her to become a Carnegie Teacher Fellow and help design the Basic School Model. The Basic School's philosophy reflects a similar commitment to adult leadership and student ownership with a curriculum that is both thematic and project based. Boyer (1995) contends and we deeply agree:

> But community doesn't just happen, even in a small school. To become a true community the institution must be organized around people. . . . What we are really talking about is the culture of the school, the vision that is shared, the ways people relate to one another. . . . Simply stated, the school becomes a community for learning when it is a purposeful place, a communicative place, a just place, a disciplined place, a caring place, and a celebrative place. (17–18)

These previous years of learning and organizing and teaching led me to Hamline University and the design and implementation of learning communities and learning circles on the masters level that is described in detail in Collay et al.'s *Learning Circles: Creating Conditions for Professional Development* (1998). We four coauthors formed a study circle and wrote the book by meeting Friday mornings for a year as a learning circle, where we were teachers and learners, collegially sharing, reflecting, and taking responsibility to influence each other, constructing and composing this book. That circle is now disbanded, but our work continues in new relationships that constitute leadership circles of learning.

We define learning circles as "small communities of learners among teachers and others who come together intentionally for the purpose of supporting each other in the process of learning." A learning community is based on these six conditions: building community, constructing knowledge, supporting learners, assessing expectations, documenting reflection, and changing culture.

Writing the essay "Learning Community" published in *Center Magazine* (1972), Joseph Schwab articulates a case for the idea of learning in community: "I propose, rather, deliberate shaping of learning situations and classroom practices, whatever the subject matter and whatever the grade level, so that they will contain as factors intrinsic to the learning process itself, certain basic components of community." Schwab's work was to impact greatly both the Holmes Group's work in teacher education reform and the establishment of the National Board for Professional Teacher Standards (1991), whose fifth proposition reads that teachers will learn professionally in "learning communities."

Linda Lambert, in her preface to *Learning Circles* (1998), notes that the power for learning circle members comes from the freedom of choice, taking responsibility for professional development, and defining your personal agendas. "As you explore and create these three freedoms (choice, responsibility, agenda setting) around shared work, you perform as a professional culture." The literature is very clear: the professional educators' work cultures are directly related to student achievement if they have these four factors in place: shared decision making, a shared sense of purpose, collaborative work toward that purpose, and collective responsibility. Those of us who think a great deal about professional development and school reform have moved beyond the notions of training or in-service for adult learning. We favor opportunities that are based on the stakeholders' intentionality: purposeful collaboration, dialogue, inquiry, leadership, and reflection.

Lambert contends that teachers represent the only significant educational group that has not been held responsible for educational reform. But here at EdVisions, we model teacher leadership and teacher ownership. We believe it is imperative, if students are to own their work and to be risk takers in learning, that the adults who lead, model, and advise student learners ought to practice what they preach and be accountable, be active learners, be active citizens, and be responsible. "To understand this imperative we must understand that leading and leadership are inextricably intertwined." To lead is to engage community or circle participants "in the process of meaning-making: the process of learning toward purpose."

Lambert argues further that the typical mistake (that we do not make at EdVisions) is to focus professional development on either child learning or self-learning. Professional learning has been centered on the self, the teacher, or the child. While the child learner and the adult self-learner are critically important, this emphasis misses the two factors that will change schools: purposeful, intentional responsibility for the learning of other adults in the culture and mutual responsibility for the learning organization, the learning community as a whole. Together, knowing your mission and vision by living it out, you create your learning community as you work to build it, living out in practice what you value. This is a fundamental belief at EdVisions and developed at MNCS; students and teachers are owners of their work.

About 150 years ago in the Minnesota river valley, "the little doctor" William Mayo organized his first medical clinic that would lead years later to his sons' founding of the Mayo Clinic in Rochester. When we were dialoguing and composing of our collaborative book *Teachers as Owners* (Dirkswager 2002), about teachers in professional practice organizations, we operated as a leadership writing circle. I became fascinated with the Mayo Clinic and its notions of professional leadership and professional development. First, the clinic leaders (administrators, managers) are the best practitioners, the best doctors. Second, doctors continue with their clinical practice. Third, they continually learn. Fourth, administrative leadership is a temporary role. Fifth, physicians began as both professionals and apprentices. Sixth, professionals work as a collaborative team. This is a good model for us—the clinical learning community—for those who believe that education is not yet the profession it could be.

Many of us at EdVisions revere the work of two learning communities that utilized learning circles. They are connected with each other; moreover, they are connected to our lives. They are the Highlander Folk School and the Citizenship Schools of the 1960s. We sometimes refer to ourselves here in Henderson as the "Midlander" or "Outlander" Center, and we view our work as active citizenship by ordinary citizens to solve public problems. The citizenship school program grew out of the work of Septima Clark and Esau Jenkins on the islands off South Carolina. Their goal was to teach illiterate adults to read and write in order to pass arduous literacy tests that authorities used to disenfranchise poorer citizens of both races. It was adopted by the Highlander Folk School, a training center for organizers and activists (including civil rights hero Rosa Parks).

Later the Southern Christian Leadership Conference (SCLC) sponsored the citizenship schools as the civil rights movement expanded in 1962 under the leadership of Dorothy Cotton and Andrew Young. From its beginnings, the strategy of citizenship schools stressed the importance of connecting voting and literacy to a dynamic conception of citizenship itself. To that end, organizers of the school avoided normal academic approaches and treated the "students" as adults who come and go as they please, bring sewing to classes, or chew tobacco. The SCLC further developed the citizenship schools training program at Dorchester, Georgia, where the curriculum included much more than the mechanics of registering and voting. Students learned how to conduct voter registration campaigns, combat illiteracy, win government benefits for the poor, and discuss the meaning of American citizenship in ways that would inspire ordinary citizens. As Dorothy Cotton put it, "They taught a whole new way of life and functioning."

Civil rights activists saw the movement as designed, in Martin Luther King's words, "to make real the promise of democracy." But democracy meant more than simply formal rights to vote. It also meant active, public problem-solving citizenship. For Cotton, "the more important participation was to be not just in the moment when the ballot was cast but in all the moments that led up to that moment." (This citizenship story is literally excerpted from *Reinventing Citizenship: The Practice of Public Work* [Boyte 1996] by the partners of the Center for Democracy and Citizenship, Humphrey Institute of Public Affairs, University of Minnesota.)

One of the techniques or, better, practices the citizenship schools used was learned at Highlander Folk School, an adult education school in Tennessee founded in 1932 to work for justice and self-determination in the worker union and civil rights movements. The founder of Highlander, Myles Horton, in his book *The Long Haul* (1989), describes the "circle" process and its rationale. "I think of an educational workshop as a circle of learners. 'Circle' is not an accidental term, for there is no head of the table at Highlander workshops; everybody sits around in a circle. The job of the staff members is to create a relaxed atmosphere in which the participants feel free to share their experiences. Then they are encouraged to analyze, learn from and build on these experiences. Like other participants in the workshops, staff members are expected to share experiences that relate to the discussions, sources of information, and alternative suggestions."

To paraphrase Horton, concerning our work with EdVisions learning communities, the best teachers of educators working in our schools are the educators themselves. They are the experts of their own experiences and problems, they come with their own ways of thinking and doing, and EdVisions staff try to stimulate their thinking and expose them to other teacher–advisers and resource people who are also doing this work of leading small schools. Think of us at best as catalytic agents to hasten the learning process. But it is most important that they learn from each other. Then, when they work in their schools, they function as a leadership learning circle to maintain and sustain their school. It is through those deliberative efforts that change in the culture will improve the lives of learners and citizens.

For Martin Luther King Jr., Myles Horton, Dorothy Cotton, and the ordinary people, especially the young people, public schools are one fundamental way to evolve the democracy and our human hood. A favorite thought from Dr. King's last sermon, "A Revolution Is Coming," captures this imperative for social justice: "The world is more and more of a neighborhood. But is it any more of a human hood? If we do not learn to live together as brothers and sisters we shall perish together as fools."

We had the opportunity in the past year to survey and interview some of the graduates of MNCS (see chapter 9). Time and again the graduates spoke of the freedom they had as learners, the respect they received from their advisers to be responsible and thereby be free. This is a special place because people took the risk to dream of, then concretely build and sustain, a learning community that would ultimately transform the lives of its stakeholders and the community around them.

Educator Joseph Schwab used to point to a double meaning to the phrase "learning community." He wrote, "In one sense, all knowledge is at bottom communal, and all learning a matter of participation in a dialogue, real or imagined. You learn the musical scales to take part in the community, past and present, of those who make and appreciate music. You are part of the community, even when playing the piano alone. The ancient Greeks emphasized the communal aspect of mathematics when they called it a performance art, linking it to such worlds as music and dance. Reading and writing and speaking are the passports to the kingdom of discourse itself, which always takes place in some kind of community" (Schwab 1972).

The second meaning Schwab observed in "learning community" is that the arts of participation are themselves attitudes, habits, and skills that need to be learned. "Particularly where the web of community is fragile and threatened, and where children encounter too few adults, community itself is something that needs to be learned." Schwab goes on to say, "In the learning community, both worlds — 'community' and 'learning' — must have equal weight. A web of mutual respect, trust, and responsibility is as important as the intellectual content of programs. Without the life of the mind, community lacks intellectual purpose; without community, academic work lacks meaning. The fusion of both can create the 'humanities' in the double sense of the word—the marriage of head and heart in human fellowship that produces true education."

Reformer Roland Barth (2001) asks a fundamental, most important question on which rests the promise of school-based reform and our future work. He writes, "How much are you prepared to risk? How much are you prepared to risk of what is familiar, comfortable, safe, and perhaps working well for you, in the name of better education for others? . . . To learn is to risk; to lead others toward profound levels of learning is to risk, to promote personal and organizational renewal is to risk; to create schools hospitable to human learning is to risk. In short the career of the lifelong learner and of the school reformer is the life of a risk taker."

At Avalon High School, I so admire the staff because they are good people and good advisers and good learners; they take risks with each other that most university folk can only dream of. They are willing to be evaluated by each other through personal reflection and accountability, by students, and by parents. It takes courage to be so vulnerable, so open to critical praise and feedback. The school's success partly results from such leadership, such risk taking while learning, advising, and teaching.

Barth (2001) then asks, "Why is the culture of risk-taking so crucial to schools of the twenty first century? Because human learning is most profound, most transformative, and most enduring when two conditions are present: when we take risks and when a safety net or belaying line supports us when we fall, so that we don't get killed. . . . Schools exist to promote and sustain profound levels of human learning. Yet neither of the two conditions most associated with human learning—risk-taking and a safety net for those who risk—are present in (most) schools. These conditions are interdependent and are at the very core of a culture hospitable to human learning." While these two conditions are not yet prevalent in most schools, they are at the heart of our EdVisions schools.

There is a diversified and growing democratic movement for creating just and sustainable schools in which the students and teachers are owners of their work, where families and teachers are partners and leaders, and where learning communities and learning circles offer a model for school reform. This reform depends on the stakeholders claiming owner-ship for what they will learn and how they will learn it. And for the teach-ers specifically, it means making their own decisions and designing expe-riences to further their professional development agenda. This demands respect, review, and reflection from caring collaborators, including stu-dents, parents, and teachers.

Over a hundred years ago, if you had visited John Dewey's Laboratory School at the University of Chicago, you would have found two assump-tions and two goals interwoven in the lived experiences of the learning community. The first assumption was that children are not merely incom-plete adults but are whole people whose primary work is living and learn-ing. The second assumption was that the living/learning conditions neces-sary for moral and mental progress is the same for the adult as it is for the child. Based on these assumptions, the goals of the living democratic lab-oratory are the development of the school as a collaborative community that would meet the social needs of students and the "intellectual devel-opment of the child through activity." Based on this perspective, the per-sonnel of EdVisions schools understand through commitment and lived experience one of Dewey's essential insights: "democracy is more than a form of government; it is primarily a mode of associated living, of con-joint communicated experience."

REFERENCES

Adler, M. (1982). *The Paideia proposal*. New York: Macmillan.

Barth, R. (1972). *Open education and the American school*. Boston: Agathon.

Barth, R. (2001). *Learning by heart*. New York: Jossey-Bass.

Boyer, E. (1995). *The basic school*. Princeton, NJ: Carnegie Foundation for the Advancement of Teaching.

Boyte, H. (1996). *Reinventing citizenship: The practice of public work*. St. Paul: University of Minnesota Extension.

Collay, M., Dunlap, D., Enloe, W., & Gagnon, G. (1998). *Learning circles: Cre-ating conditions for professional development*. Thousand Oaks, CA: Corwin Press.

Dewey, J. (1997). *Democracy and education*. New York: Free Press.

Dirkswager, E., ed. (2002). *Teachers as owners: A key to revitalizing American education* . Lanham, MD: ScarecrowEducation, 2002.

Enloe, W. (1996). *Creating Context*. Tuscon, AZ: Zephyr Press.

Enloe, W. (2002). *Lessons from ground zero: A Hiroshima and Nagasaki story*. St. Paul, MN: Hamline University Press.

Enloe, W., & Morris, R. (2003). *Nagasaki spirits, Hiroshima voices*. St. Paul, MN: Hamline University Press.

Gardner, H. (1973). *The quest for mind: Piaget, Levi-Strauss and the structuralist movement*. New York: Knopf.

Horton, M. (1989). *The long haul: An autobiography*. New York: Teachers College Press.

Kohl, H. (1969). *The open classroom*. New York: Basic Books.

Piaget, J. (1973). The right to education in the present world. In *To understand is to invent: The future of education*. New York: Grossman Publishers.

Piaget, J. (1974). The genesis of the new methods. In *Science of education and the psychology of the child*. New York: Penguin Putnam.

Schwab, J. (1972). Learning community. In *Center Magazine*.

6

Democratic Circles

Darrol Bussler

"Josh attends this school because it's like a Quaker meeting." This was the quick but thoughtful response the mother of an Avalon student gave to me when I inquired about the reasons her family had chosen Avalon School. She said no more; she didn't have to. Her simple comment communicated what she perceived as positive practices based on positive principles at the school of their choice.

For those not acquainted with Quaker beliefs and practices, the parent's response may not provide a sufficient explanation about the "democratic way of life" that is a foundation of schools such as Avalon. This chapter provides a discussion about the principles that inform practices at EdVisions schools. A fivefold framework is offered, and the italicized words identify the five sections to follow: our 1) *social* nature results in 2) interactive *relationships*, guided by 3) principles of *democracy*, reflecting 4) *restorative* practices such as 5) the *circle* process.

SOCIAL BY NATURE

A primary research base for work in EdVisions is that of Peter Kropotkin, a Russian who carried out his extensive, holistic research on insects, birds, mammals, and humans over a century ago and published his results in 1902 in *Mutual Aid*. Kropotkin's title indicates a social orientation, and the thesis of his book provides a framework for how the work of EdVisions schools may be viewed:

> The greater the sociability of a species,
>   the greater its intelligence;
>   the greater its intelligence,
>   the greater its chance for survival.

The more we are social, relating and communicating with each other, the smarter we can become; and the smarter we become, the greater chance we have to succeed. Kropotkin's thesis focuses on the social nature of all the species he studied; more specifically, Kropotkin observed relating and communicating—being social. Relating and communicating with each other is basic in the governance of EdVisions schools along with the teaching and learning practices.

Kropotkin's thesis is reflected in the practices of EdVisions schools; we are conscious of the fact that we are social by nature; thus, we do not focus on formal teaching of social skills; we live them. We talk. EdVisions schools are not "quiet schools"; they are not "sh" schools; rather, the basis of governance and learning is being in relationship and speaking with one another.

The sociability disposition is evident in its most basic form in "check-ins," which are modeled at the EdVisions staff meetings. Every meeting or gathering begins with a check-in when each staff member briefly shares a personal or professional experience, thought, or feeling that is important to that staff member at that particular moment. These quick individual check-ins, often less than a minute, may include incidents such as getting a traffic ticket on the way to the meeting, being up all night with a sick child, having a wedding in the family last weekend, experiencing the death of a friend, seeing a fantastic movie, or having a positive experience or insight in one of the EdVisions schools. These check-ins are a reminder, first and foremost, that we are human, that we are whole persons bringing our personal and professional lives to the table. A grandmother of a student recently noted that in some organizations, "The professionals are so professional that they forget they're human." Check-ins are a means for us to connect with one another on a basic human level: we are persons first and then professionals.

Staff members of EdVisions schools are encouraged to use check-ins in their meetings and gatherings. We find that staffs that invest time through this simple activity or similar processes they identify tend to have healthy relationships and are productive. Advisers are encouraged to implement check-ins with their advisory groups; this is often done when the group assembles for the first time during the week. Some advisers use the check-in at the beginning as well as a reflection at the end of every day. The social process is a means to develop relationships between students, between advisers and students, and between advisers. Because we are conscious of our social nature, we seek to develop relationships that are interactive.

RELATIONSHIPS: BASIC TO CONTENT AND INTERACTIVE

The check-in process reflects a view held by Larry Cuban of Stanford University, who contends that "relationship is basic to content." EdVisions advisers are aware that if learning is to take place, it will more likely occur at a higher level if healthy relationships exist in the advisory groups and the school as a whole. We believe in getting our relationship house in order, first, as part of the processes of governance and learning. We believe, as John Dewey expressed a century ago, that learning is a social process. And social processes lead to interactive relationships.

While the research of Kropotkin in the 1800s provides a research base for our social practices, it is the recent literature in quantum physics that supports us in our views regarding the importance of relationships. Physicists such as Margaret Wheatley, Myron Kellner-Rogers, and Fritjof Capra emphasize the importance of relationship. Wheatley, in *Leadership and the New Science* (1999), writes, "In the quantum world, relationships are not just interesting; to many physicists, they are *all* there is to reality" (34).

Capra holds the same view in *The Web of Life* (1996), his title indicating the connectedness and interdependence of all. In his discussions of sustainability, Capra proposes "the basic principles of ecology and use[s] them as guidelines to build sustainable human communities." The first principle he proposes is interdependence. "All members of an ecological community are interconnected in a vast and intricate network of relationships, the web of life. They derive their essential properties and, in fact, their very existence from their relationships to other things. Interdependence—the *mutual* [same view as Kropotkin] dependence of all life processes on one another—is the nature of all ecological relationships. The behavior of every living member of the ecosystem depends on the behavior of many others. The success of the whole community depends on the success of its individual members, while the success of each member depends on the success of the community as a whole" (298). Relationship serves as a guiding principle for EdVisions.

When I was invited to work with EdVisions, the theme of the conversation was one word: *relationship*. The reason was clear; the reason remains clear. When relationships are functioning in healthy ways, a school is productive; when relationships are dysfunctional, the level of productivity reflects the dysfunction. If we agree with the quantum physicists, we could conclude that we are all in continual relationship, whether we are conscious of it or not. However, "being social" and "being in relationship," in and of itself, does not guarantee anything. The murder that occurred just ten blocks from my home recently was a result of a social process and relationship gone wrong. What guides our social processes and the development of our relationships in EdVisions? The response of the student's mother at Avalon implies these principles. Our discussion moves to a review of the principles that guide our behaviors.

DEMOCRATIC PRINCIPLES: GUIDING BEHAVIORS

Shortly after my association with EdVisions began, I suggested that our work be guided by values. My belief in the power of values as a guide for behaviors developed over a number of years as a public school teacher and as a community education director in a first-ring suburban community.

My belief in the power of values guiding behaviors was unexpectedly clarified and reinforced while I was a tourist at Disney World; my first visit was to Epcot. I immediately became aware of something unusual: cast member (employee) behaviors were consistent and produced consistent results. The results were smiles, laughter, and fun times for tourists like me. My curiosity gave way. While taking my "trip around the world," I simultaneously took a research trip around Epcot and then the Magic Kingdom, interviewing over twenty-five cast members about their training.

The responses were consistently the same: seven principles informed the cast members about behaviors expected of them. Some of the cast members were carrying the principles on business-size cards in their pockets; others had them taped next to their cash registers. Again and again, I saw smiles at Disney; I joined in, experiencing fun as a result of employees carrying out behaviors based on specific principles:

1. Establish eye contact/smile.
2. Greet and welcome.
3. Seek out guest contact.
4. Provide immediate service recovery.
5. Display appropriate body language.
6. Preserve the magical experience.
7. Thank each and every guest.

But I wanted to be sure about my conclusions regarding Disney. A year later, I participated in the seminar "The Disney Approach to Leadership Excellence" (2001) and found my nugget—the Disney formula: *Values = Behaviors*. It is a simple formula, requiring no mathematic or scientific skills. The formula simply invites us to be conscious of our behaviors—knowing why we do what we do. And for a moment, we return to the thoughts of our quantum physicists who recognize our most basic human qualities. Wheatley and Kellner-Rogers, in *A Simpler Way* (1996), contend, "An emergent world invites us to use our most human of all capacities, our consciousness" (75). The process of identifying values for EdVisions was a conscious one in which we identified some common beliefs that could guide our practice. We want to be conscious about what we do.

Four values were identified as the common values of EdVisions: reform, project-based learning, accountability, and democracy. The first was easy; EdVisions is about change in schooling, both in governance and in the teaching–learning process. The second, project-based learning, related to the first; the Minnesota New Country School's experience in project-based learning was to be replicated. The third, accountability, was a reminder to carry out the first two values. And the fourth, democracy, was inherent in the very structure of a teacher-owned model as well as individual learning within a community of learners.

Democracy was identified as a value to remind us that democracy is more than merely principles or values. It is a "way of life." This concept is not new. I was first introduced to it when reading the 1926 publication by T. V. Smith and Eduard C. Lindeman titled *The Democratic Way of Life.* I was struck with the idea that democracy is more than a political structure, more than knowledge and skills in family, school, and community living; it is a disposition—a way of being. It is a way of life. What explains this way of life? What can help us understand it as a way of life? Several sources, both historical and recent, can inform.

The French Revolution slogan provides simple guidance for our work: *liberté, egalité, fraternité.* Democracy means that there is liberty—freedom to make choices; project-based learning is all about individual choices. And with this freedom comes equality—equal opportunity for others to choose. And the behaviors resulting from these two values can, and often do, become the basis for our conflicts. What happens if my choice interferes with the choice of another? This conflict moves us to the third value in the French slogan: *fraternité*, or "community." When the choices of individuals result in conflict, a community process becomes the means to resolve the conflict. And it takes us back to the earlier discussion on sociability; in order to resolve the conflict, we have to talk. We practice social democracy.

I recall an education-related experience that simply but powerfully modeled these values and continues to remind me about the practicality of the three values in the French slogan. I was facilitating a community development process in a small western Minnesota village and had introduced the French slogan early on in the process. It was apparent that many community members remembered it from their history lessons. The meeting was in the back room of the local coffee shop, filled with citizens. One of the issues facing this community and a neighboring community was the perception of the need to consolidate their schools. The problem was that each village wanted the high school in their village. Each village made their choice; the choices were obviously in conflict. During the discussion, a retired farmer with a cap pulled over his forehead and sitting in the back of the room said, "Well, it seems to me that we gotta remember the French slogan. It seems to me we just gotta talk to each other." This retired and thoughtful farmer understood the very basis of democracy:

speaking to each other, using sociability to solve conflicts, making decisions, and practicing social democracy. The social democratic process is especially crucial in the governance structure in EdVisions Schools, along with the project-based approach with advisory structures.

Of course, conflict is a natural element in all these processes. The framework for working through these conflicts is guided by two democratic values: the value of the individual and the simultaneous value of community. In *Democracy and Education* (1916), Dewey identified the two components that challenged democracy: meeting the interests and needs of the individual and meeting the needs of the group. The challenge for advisers and students in EdVisions schools is to recognize the value of both the individual through project-based learning and the value of the advisory group of which individuals are members. It is a laboratory experience in learning to experience the relationships between liberty, equality, and fraternity. If Dewey were observing an EdVisions school, he would probably say that the school is developing democratic citizens. The school, according to Dewey, would be meeting its primary mission.

In order to ensure that students are being prepared as democratic citizens, advisers encourage students to "do democracy daily." How is this achieved? By developing processes that ascertain that every student can experience four skills necessary in the democratic way of life. These skills include 1) speaking, 2) listening, 3) making positive decisions for self, and 4) making positive decisions with others. Processes that provide the opportunities to practice these skills in authentic ways are made possible through daily check-ins mentioned previously as well as through restorative practices, utilized in situations where negative conflicts exist.

RESTORATIVE PRACTICES: NO TOLERANCE RATHER THAN ZERO TOLERANCE

Restorative practices in schools, sometime referred to as restorative measures, are an outgrowth of restorative justice in the criminal justice system. I was first introduced to restorative justice when my house was vandalized by two neighborhood boys. When the police informed me that they had apprehended two suspects, I recall making a decision that I would work *with* those who had harmed me.

My first intent was to restore myself since my immediate behaviors, like behaviors of most victims of crime, reflected a loss of control in my life. My second intent was to address the fear in our neighborhood through a restorative process that would include restoring our youth back into the neighborhood. One of the processes we utilized was having the two boys, who had harmed me and the neighborhood, help me prepare and serve a dinner for all our neighbors in my home. This process was based on a belief in accountability, that is, holding the boys accountable for their behaviors, and a belief in the power of having those who harm others face those they have harmed. Thirty-five neighborhood residents gathered in my home and were served by the two boys and myself. The result was healing rather than hurt, security rather than fear, restoration rather than revenge, and learning rather than punishment.

Principles of restorative practices are closely related and in some cases identical to the principles already discussed in this chapter. Restorative practices are based on social processes; they are value based; they are democratic. The following statements from *Restorative Measures*, a publication by the Minnesota Department of Children, Families and Learning (1996), provide a basic explanation. The first provides a philosophic perspective:

> Consistent use of restorative measures represents a philosophic shift. For some this may be a shift from perceiving some students as a problem to actually being able to identify their strengths and potential for success. For others it may be a change in how behavioral problems are handled. Expanding or beginning restorative measures means getting everyone to agree with the idea of restoration rather than punishment or control models of behavioral management. Restorative measures also means respecting that all affected parties have the ability to contribute to the solution. Once people are informed and understand the guiding principles, they can begin to think of a myriad of applications. (9)

In EdVisions schools, discipline issues are not viewed as opportunities to apply automatic punishment since we believe in the original meaning of discipline, that is, to learn. We recognize and value the research results found in sociology: punishment does not change long-term behaviors.

This view is the basis for restorative measures as explained by the Department of Children, Families and Learning:

> Punishment often has the effect of further discouraging and controlling someone who needs encouragement and self-control. Restorative measures repair harm and rebuild relationships rather than simply seeking punishment, expulsion, shame or revenge. Restorative results are measured by how much repair is done rather than by how much punishment was inflicted. Restitution to those harmed becomes the rule, not the exception. Given when harm is done to those directly victimized, to the community and to those who did the harm, all parties in restorative measures have input into how to make things right. (7)

A comparison of retributive and restorative processes can quickly inform:

Retributive Practices	**Restorative Practices**
View misbehaviors as danger and threat	View misbehaviors as danger and threat with opportunity
Compete against each other	Cooperate with each other
Demand respect	Show respect, authenticity
Do something *to* student	Do something *with* student
Tell the student	Speak and listen *with* the student
Remove the student	Seek to reintegrate the student for learning
Control the student	Support the student to control self
Solve the problem *for* the student	Support the student to solve the problem *with* others: peers/ teachers/family
Use head: think	Use head and heart: think and feel
Focus on rules and punishment: be absolutist (black and white)	Focus on learning: be situational (gray)
Use behaviorist methods: rewards and punishment	Use restorative methods: circles, group conferencing, mediation; restore right relationships with accountability and responsibility

A prime characteristic of restorative practices is that it is situation based. It requires thinking, not merely following someone else's predetermined, uninformed rule. The previous comparison can give insight into a comparison of zero-tolerance and no-tolerance policies:

Zero Tolerance	**No Tolerance**
Harm is taken seriously	Harm is taken seriously
Specific consequences applied uniformly: detention, isolation, suspension, and expulsion are common consequences	Variety of consequences are available: circles, restitution, family group conferencing, community/school service as well as suspension and expulsion
Consequences are specific and based on predetermined rules	Consequences are situational and based on circumstances—what is most effective for all involved
More equitable than fair	More fair than equitable
Letter of the law followed	Spirit and intent of the law followed
Education on how to change behavior may be part of consequences, i.e., anger management, conflict resolution	Education on how to change behavior may be part of consequence, i.e., anger management, conflict resolution with support to change

—Adapted from Minnesota Department of Children, Families, and Learning (1996)

It is important to note that a no-tolerance policy is democratic based. First, no tolerance provides due process; everyone has the right to present their view. All must be heard. Since more options are available in a no-tolerance policy, a social decision-making process is required; all talk, all listen, all decide. A process that includes all these characteristics and provides an opportunity "to do democracy" is the circle process.

CIRCLE PROCESS: SOCIAL DEMOCRACY

The circle process is the most social democratic process I have learned. It can be used for behavioral issues discussed in the preceding section as well as for learning, informing, and understanding. The process, based on American Indian practices, includes simple guidelines that can be applied in any setting with any age. A "circle keeper" guides the process, including an explanation of guidelines after opening the circle.

1. After a circle is formed, participants pass a talking piece from participant to participant; the talking piece provides the holder the opportunity to speak while others listen. Individuals always have the right not to speak—to pass. The talking piece is passed clockwise—a Native American practice to remind participants to be in tune with natural movements of the universe.
2. Participants are invited to speak from the heart—being honest, saying what they mean, and meaning what they say.
3. Participants are invited to speak in a good way—no name calling, no swearing, and no put-downs.
4. Participants stay in circle until it is decided to break or to conclude.
5. The circle process is open, not closed. Confidentiality is expected while mandated reporting remains in effect. Permission to share information outside of circle may be requested.

Circles may be used for check-ins. Circles may be used by advisers in learning processes to provide each an opportunity to contribute verbally. Circles may be used in meetings to ensure that all participants have the opportunity to speak; the circle process can be especially effective when emotions are intense, when individuals are stepping on each other's words, when shouting and verbal abuse is present, or when a few monopolize the discussion. A talking piece can restore a democratic process.

The restorative process of circles reminds participants that they are members of a community where democracy is a way of life—all *do* democracy:

• All have opportunity to speak
• All have responsibility to listen
• All have opportunity to made individual decisions (speak or pass)
• All have the opportunity to make decisions with each other

Jean Shinoda Bolen, in *The Millionth Circle* (1999), reminds us that the circle is a principal as well as a shape.

FROM "BY NATURE TO "LIVING NATURALLY"

The opening section of this chapter began with a reference to the sociability that is characteristic of species that survive in great numbers: We are social *by nature*. The concluding section, the Circle Process, offers a method that is in harmony, in a compatible relationship with what we are by nature; the circle has us *living naturally*.

I have often experimented with this compatibility. The results are always consistent; they never vary. When working with a group, I ask them to form smaller groups of approximately the same numbers and to form single lines to play Follow the Leader. I inform them that when a bell sounds, they are to stop and listen for directions.

After a brief time playing Follow the Leader, I ring the bell and ask them to analyze questions about the game. After they hear the questions, they re-form their lines, naturally, into circles, without being told to do so. All groups have done this every time in every experiment I have conducted for the past ten years. All groups naturally move from straight lines to circles. When asked why they do this, they tell me that they do it because they can see and hear everyone, so everyone can participate.

The results remind us about our sociability and how we naturally move to the principle of the circle. We are born social—we are social by nature. Our teaching and learning processes can, naturally, reflect what we are by nature, and as Bolen states in *The Millionth Circle*, "every important relationship is a universe of two. Even though there are only two people in it, you are either in a circle or a hierarchy" (17). EdVisions encourages schools to be in conscious relationships, to choose to be in circle.

Christina Baldwin, in *Calling the Circle* (1998, 206), cites Paula Underwood, an American Indian, whose words serve as a call to the democratic way of life in EdVisions schools. Underwood's words take us back to our opening story of the mother at Avalon School who stated that the family chose Avalon because "it's like a Quaker meeting":

THE PEOPLE
  Formed a circle round the Fire,
        each showing an attentive face
        to every other person.

AND THEY SPOKE
  each waiting quietly
   til the other had finished,
  as they had learned to do,
   a circle of silent listening
  framing the wisdom each contained
   until the wisdom of all was spoken,
  contained at last
    by the Circle of the People.
Thinking now
  of the quiet circle of listening hearts,
   they were filled with understanding
   of the value of their way.
AND A FIRM RESOLVE SWEPT THROUGH THEM.
THEY DECIDED
  To be a People
   who would perpetuate and refine
   this manner of ordered council
    which they had achieved.

REFERENCES

Baldwin, C. (1998). *Calling the circle: The first and future culture*. New York: Bantam Books.

Bolen, J. S. (1999). *The millionth circle*. Berkeley, CA: Conari Press.

Capra, F. (1996). *The web of life*. New York: Anchor Books.

Dewey, J. (1916). *Democracy and education: An introduction to the philosophy of education*. New York: Macmillan.

The Disney approach to leadership excellence. (2001). Seminar. Disney Institute, Orlando, FL.

Kropotkin, P. (1902). *Mutual aid: A factor in evolution*. London: William Heinemann, Fourth Impression, April 1910.

Minnesota Department of Children, Families, and Learning. (1996). *Restorative measures*. St. Paul, MN: Office of Community Service.

Smith, T. V., & Lindeman, E. C. (1926). *The democratic way of life*. New York: New American Library.

Wheatley, M. (1999). *Leadership and the new science*. San Francisco: Berrett-Koehler Publishers.

Wheatley, M. J., & Kellner-Rogers, M. (1996). *A simpler way*. San Francisco: Berrett-Koehler Publishers.

Experiential Learning: Why Project-Based Learning Works

Scott Wurdinger

At a K–12 curriculum advisory committee meeting, I was handed a report containing information on various standardized tests students are required to take in the school district where I reside. The number was overwhelming. "The explosion in testing, particularly high stakes testing, over the past two decades has put enormous weight on tests and has placed them squarely in the center of schooling" (Rothman 2001, 431). High schools, colleges, and universities continue to use paper and pencil tests as the primary tool to measure intelligence.

Students are inundated by tests, which unfortunately promotes the use of lectures as a primary teaching method resulting in a learning process based primarily on memorization. It appears that teachers are continuing to rely heavily on abstract subjects and passive methods of learning, whereas students prefer active methods (Levine and Cureton 1998). The dichotomy between how students learn best and how educators teach is not new. Dewey mentioned this idea as early as 1916, when he stated, "Formal instruction, on the contrary, easily becomes remote and dead-abstract and bookish, to use the ordinary words of depreciation" (8).

It appears that tests and more passive methods of learning will continue for at least the next several years; "the new legislation, reauthorizing the Elementary and Secondary Education Act (ESEA), will tie federal education funding to improvements in student test scores (Heinecke, Curry-Corcoran, and Moon 2003, 7). Schools that do not meet specific standards run the risk of losing federal funding, which will most likely result in a situation where teachers spend most of their time "teaching to the tests."

Fortunately, schools like the Minnesota New Country School (MNCS) are implementing innovative teaching and learning strategies that provide students and teachers with an experiential approach to education, allowing them opportunities to determine what they want to learn and how they want to learn it, to be creative problem solvers, and, in the end, to apply what they are learning. The purpose of this chapter is to discuss why the experiential learning process, which is the learning theory used with project-based learning, is so effective.

TWO VIEWS ON EXPERIENTIAL LEARNING

One common view of experiential learning consists of a sequential process with different components, and learning occurs once one has completed all the components in the sequence. Dewey (1916), one of the earliest theorists to discuss a learning sequence, proposed that an educative experience occurs when one identifies a problem, observes the variables associated with the problem, develops a plan, and tests this plan against reality to discover a solution. The testing phase requires the learner to apply information, which is the key component of experiential learning. Students involved in project-based learning rely heavily on this view of experiential learning. Students create projects and activities that require them to develop plans, solve unexpected problems that may arise, and implement their ideas to complete them.

I see this process in action frequently in several of the experiential education graduate courses I teach. Two courses in particular are designed specifically as project-based courses where students plan, design, and implement their projects over the course of a semester. Developing new curricula and teaching methods are common projects in these courses. Since many of the students are actually teachers, these courses provide them with opportunities to explore new ideas and develop new ways of doing things in their classrooms. Planning, designing, and implementing these new ideas requires them to think their way through the experiential learning process. Teachers often realize at the conclusion of their projects that this approach to learning may be also beneficial for their own students, and so they begin utilizing this approach more often in their classrooms.

Experiential learning has also been viewed as learning that occurs outside traditional classroom settings. "Experiential learning is a broad spectrum of educational experiences, such as community service, field work, sensitivity training groups, internships, cooperative education involving work in business or industry, and undergraduate participation in faculty research" (McKeachie 1999, 154). This view identifies experiential learning as a place outside the four walls of a classroom where students engage in a variety of learning experiences. Project-based learning relies heavily on this view as well because students must leave the classroom and experience things in a variety of different environments in order to complete their projects.

These two views suggest that experiential learning is a process that often occurs away from traditional classroom settings. Project-based learning weaves these two views of experiential learning together, allowing students to develop problem-solving skills while completing their projects and activities outside the four walls of a classroom. Students develop plans, address questions and problems that arise, and test their ideas in real-world situations, which is similar to Dewey's previously mentioned learning sequence. Project-based learning utilizes the principles of experiential learning because it "emphasizes student interest rather than following a fixed curriculum, emphasizes a broad, interdisciplinary focus rather than a narrow, discipline-based focus; uses direct, primary, or original sources rather than texts, lectures, and secondary sources; emphasizes data and materials developed by students rather than teachers" (Newell 2003, 5). These are some of the key components that make experiential learning unique and effective.

STUDENT INTEREST

Student interest is critical to experiential learning processes. When students are given freedom to design their own projects, they have a tendency to take more ownership in their learning (this concept is discussed in greater detail by Newell in chapter 3). This often presents a situation where motivation becomes intrinsic. A student creates a project based on an interest and is motivated to complete the project because it has relevancy to his or her life. Desire is internal and propels the student forward in the learning process. It is the catalyst that ignites learning and carries the student to the completion of the project.

Students are less likely to see the relevancy when subjects are compartmentalized and what is to be learned is not necessarily of their interest but of the teacher's or school's interest. When interest is internal as opposed to being forced, students become emotionally and intellectually invested in the learning process. Dewey noted, "Interest is in the closest relation to the emotional life, on one side; and through its close relation . . . to the intellectual life, on the other side" (1973, 422). Educators must tap into the student's emotional side in order to initiate the learning process. It appears that the primary aim of formal education is often focused on absorbing content, which tends to sever emotions from the learning process, resulting in a lack of desire and motivation. When students choose projects that are of value to them, they become excited and pursue learning on their own. In essence, they become self-directed learners.

Interest is critical at the outset of the learning process, but educators may need to guide the process so that interest continues throughout the duration of the project. When students are able to visualize their end view or goal, they can direct their efforts toward achieving this end. The means used to reach this end may require students to undergo a series of trials and errors before they accomplish the task or complete the project. It is during the trial-and-error phase that educators may need to provide information and resources that will allow students to overcome barriers they face. Otherwise, students may lose interest, choosing to create another project that may have similar results.

Educators can foster the learning process by asking meaningful questions and provide appropriate challenges that will help maintain interest. Not enough challenge may result in boredom, and too much challenge may result in frustration. In either situation, learning may cease if the educator does not provide appropriate guidance. This does not mean that educators should provide the answers when students get stuck; rather, they should provide resources that will allow students to move forward in their search for solutions. Rather than providing data to be memorized for a test, this process allows students to make mistakes and learn to solve problems as a result of those mistakes.

Though this process is frequently arduous and will require time because students may make numerous mistakes along the way, the learning may ultimately have greater meaning. Educators should place equal emphasis on the means and the ends. Projects, as opposed to worksheets and other academic exercises, tap into students' interests and allow them to work through a problem-solving process in order to complete their goals.

DEFINING KNOWLEDGE

Gardner (1993) identified six different ways to learn, which implies that individuals may be more adept with one style of learning over others. For instance, one may be more adept with the linguistic style and less adept with bodily-kinesthetic. And although an individual may be more adept with linguistic rather than kinesthetic, he or she may need to use both in order to solve certain problems. The nature of reality requires us to solve problems, and solving problems requires a combination of thinking and doing. In many cases it requires the use of our bodies.

The six learning styles may help us identify our learning preferences, but life requires us to use multiple styles. Whether it is training a dog, raising a child, fixing a car, or writing a book, they all entail using knowledge to solve problems. We think and then test our ideas to discover solutions. Experiential learning combines theory with experience and mirrors reality because it requires individuals to solve problems by applying information. The process begins in the present and moves the student into the future toward the unknown.

Projects and activities require students to solve problems and search for solutions that allow them to be discoverers of knowledge. A project is developed based on an interest. A search begins that includes solving problems that arise, and a process of thinking and doing occurs almost simultaneously that allows students to discover answers otherwise unknown to them. This process requires students to think for themselves and solve real-life problems. Most occupations require problem-solving skills; however, traditional education often emphasizes the skill of memorization. When educators start in the present but then move backward to the past by asking students to remember information that others have already discovered, this implies that knowledge is static. Students in traditional education settings are often provided with the answers rather than questions and problems. Caine and Caine (2001) describe the traditional education process as follows: "Raising standards tends to mean adding more and more to the prescribed curriculum; improving teaching tends to mean ensuring that more and more teachers follow a prescribed methodology; and holding teachers and schools accountable tends to mean allocating rewards or punishments according to how well students do on standardized tests" (4).

Knowledge in this context implies that the more you can remember the smarter you are. Problem solving is not required in this theory of knowledge; however, once students leave school and enter the job market, they are expected to think for themselves and solve problems. In school they memorize theory, but in society they are expected to apply it. These are very different theories of knowledge. The process of planning, observing, testing, and reflecting is much more encompassing than sitting passively remembering information. Experiential learning requires students to get up out of their chairs and test out their own ideas in real-life situations. For instance, how can one learn to be an effective teacher without actually teaching? The definition of knowledge must include direct experience because "a theory apart from an experience cannot be definitely grasped even as theory" (Dewey 1916, 144).

Projects and activities require students to explore the unknown. The starting point is a question or problem that leads the student into the world searching for answers and solutions. Knowledge in this context is dynamic. Much knowledge changes over time, which is why the learning process should start at the present and move forward, allowing students opportunities to solve problems so they may become self-directed learners before entering the job world.

Some educators assume that younger students learn differently than adults and are not intellectually capable of engaging in a more involved theory of knowledge. Wald and Castleberry (2000) identify the following five assumptions that they suggest are unique to adult learning: "inquiry into underlying assumptions deepens the learning process, learning is an active process that occurs over time, learning is driven by the learner around meaningful issues, learning is experimental by nature, and learning is fueled by rich, diverse, accessible sources of information" (9). These assumptions imply that younger students learn differently, yet one could argue that these five assumptions are common to all learners. Problems will vary tremendously in degree of difficulty, but the process is the same.

For instance, my wife, who formerly taught fifth grade, told me a story about her school's science teacher who helped students build a device to pull balls and objects off the school roof. He started the project by asking students what was one of their most significant problems they faced at their school. Most agreed that it was frustrating to wait for custodians to get the ladder out to retrieve these objects off the roof. Students, along with the guidance of their teacher, designed and built the retrieval device to solve their problem. The problem was relatively simplistic in nature, but the process required a lot of planning, thinking, and doing before they were satisfied with the end product.

Similarly, in higher education it appears that professors often assume undergraduates learn differently than graduate students. Undergraduates are not viewed as self-directed learners, so classes are usually more structured. Yet graduate students are often given the freedom to pursue their own learning and are more readily allowed to engage in experiential learning opportunities. If educators want students to be thinkers rather than memorizers, they must embrace a theory of knowledge that is dynamic and allows all students freedom to plan and apply their ideas to solve problems that are relevant to their individual lives.

INTERDISCIPLINARY CURRICULUM

Whitehead (1929) may have been one of the earliest philosophers to reject the separation of subject matter into individual classes and support the use of an interdisciplinary curriculum; "Our modern system, with its insistence on a preliminary general education, and with its easy toleration of the analysis of knowledge into distinct subjects, is an equally unrhythmic collection of distracting scraps. I am pleading that we shall endeavor to weave in the learner's mind a harmony of patterns, by coordinating the various elements of instruction into subordinate cycles each of intrinsic worth for the immediate apprehension of the pupil" (21).

When subject matters are compartmentalized, learning may become disjointed and quickly lose meaning. In a system that designates math for fifty minutes, followed by history, then science, then English, and so on until the end of the school day, students are left wondering how it all connects and what personal purpose is served. High-stakes tests place teachers in a situation where they must provide students with very specific content. This situation does not provide incentive or the necessary time to help students connect one content area to others. Lesson plans often have specific objectives, such as learn a formula, remember dates of battles, or write a haiku poem. Such objectives are much easier to assess than whether a student has learned to think critically and solve real-life problems.

But life does not consist of segmented subject matter; rather, it requires individuals to use an interdisciplinary approach when solving problems. Marzano (1992) states that "what we know about learning indicates that instruction focusing on large, interdisciplinary curricular themes is the most effective way to promote learning" (ix). For instance, a project such as building a deck requires knowledge of a variety of subject areas. One will need to use math to calculate the number of board feet needed as well as determining costs for all materials. An individual will need to learn mechanical skills such as how to operate power drills and saws. One may also need to apply for a permit with the city and therefore understand what codes to follow. One will also need some architectural knowledge concerning structural integrity. The overall objective will require knowledge about a variety of subjects as well as the ability to connect them together in order to complete the project.

Unfortunately, many schools would have the tendency to take each of these subjects and create narrow objectives, such as learn how to operate a power drill, learn how to figure board feet, learn how to fill out a building permit application, determine the price of all the materials, and so on. When individual objectives are not connected to a relevant practical problem, they may lose their meaning and become forgotten. Life is filled with challenging problems, and projects inherently require individuals to solve a variety of problems stemming from the learning process. Experiential learning utilizes an interdisciplinary approach to education. When students directly experience a project or activity, they are exposed to a variety of subjects that are linked together. This process does not compartmentalize knowledge; instead, it allows students opportunities to connect subject matter, ultimately acknowledging the bigger picture of an interconnected world.

PRIMARY AND SECONDARY EXPERIENCES

As a former professor of undergraduate education, I had opportunities to experiment with different teaching approaches. One semester I decided to take a "theory first" approach in my team-building course. I began the semester with a series of book readings and discussions about theories associated with building teams and how to become an effective facilitator of this process. Readings focused on topics such as facilitation skills, group dynamics, and debriefing techniques.

During the first eight classes, students read and discussed these topics, and during the last eight classes, students were in the field practicing these skills with each other and with high school students. One problem with this approach was the difficulty in holding discussions during the first eight classes because many of the students had no previous experience facilitating teams. This became evident when I asked them why they were having a difficult time discussing the material, and most responded by stating that the readings did not mean anything to them. They could not make sense of the theoretical information without having some prior experience with team-building activities. I used a variety of discussion techniques mentioned in Brookfield and Preskill's book *Discussion as a Way of Teaching* (1999) without much success.

The book is filled with suggestions for generating discussion. However, these techniques are ineffective with undergraduate students who often lack direct experience. The book readings in my team-building course were not understood at the time when they were assigned because students lacked direct experience with this topic. The most common theme in my semester evaluations was that students would have to go back and reread the books because the theories did not make sense to them at the outset of the course.

This personal experience prompted me to switch the sequence and take an "experience first" approach by beginning the course with a series of hands-on experiences followed by readings and discussions. The following semester students experienced various team-building activities and practiced facilitating these activities during the first eight classes. This approach proved to be much more effective because when we began the discussions during the latter part of the semester, students were lively and excited. Many even took issue and debated some of the theories found in the books. Brookfield and

Preskill's discussion techniques were much more effective with this group of students because they could relate to the theory.

It was obvious through evaluations and class discussions that students enjoyed the primary experience portion of the course. By having it initially, they were better able to understand theoretical information (secondary sources) when it was presented. Dewey (1973) explains it this way: "the subject matter of primary experience sets the problems and furnishes the data of the first reflection which constructs the secondary objects . . . it is also obvious that test and verification of the latter is secured only by return to things of crude or macroscopic experience" (254). When students begin the learning process with a primary experience, it allows them to reflect and connect secondary sources or theoretical information to the experience, which in turn can be used to improve on future primary experiences.

Primary experience, which is necessary when completing projects, demonstrates the need for theory. Students will need to gather information and develop a theory or plan to complete their projects. For instance, in one of my graduate courses, students design and implement a project that will create a change in their work environment. The project initiates the learning process. Students spend time in class discussing and reflecting on the project with their classmates, which provides them with ideas and theories on how to improve on their project.

Experiential learning allows students to continually go back and forth between primary and secondary experience. Unlike my undergraduate courses mentioned previously, students engaged in project-based learning are free to go back and forth between the theory and experience whenever necessary to complete the project. Students do not have to wait until the next class period or the end of a school year before finding opportunities to apply their book learning. With project-based learning, there does not have to be a time lag between primary and secondary experiences. Students may acquire information through books and articles in the morning and apply it in the afternoon.

MOVING TOWARD THE FUTURE

Much of the literature on experiential learning comes from fields within higher education. Undergraduate and graduate programs in outdoor education use this learning process because students learn outdoor skills by directly participating in them. Adult education uses this process because adults prefer to be active learners, and service learning uses it because students learn about themselves and others through direct experiences with citizens in their communities. Why is there such a lack of literature regarding the use of experiential learning with high school students? Barriers seem to be mounting; less time, more structure, less money, more tests. There is little reason or incentive for high school teachers to attempt to change teaching methods that promote passive learning when classroom accountability depends heavily on high test scores.

Some educators are challenging traditional teaching methods by abandoning traditional systems and creating new ones that allow for more experiential learning. For instance, Dennis Littky, who helped create the Metropolitan School (MET), designed an experiential curriculum with internships, projects, and exhibitions that has been highly successful with its first senior class of 46 students receiving "a total of 90 acceptance letters from Brown, Reed, Northeastern, Worcester Polytech, University of Rhode Island, Community College of Rhode Island, and 20 other colleges from Vermont to Arizona" (Levine 2002, 132).

It is unfortunate that school reformers are leaving traditional education settings in order to create meaningful change because the masses are in traditional settings. Perhaps as schools such as the MET and MNCS continue to prove their effectiveness, traditional schools will take notice and begin implementing more experiential learning opportunities. As Dewey (1938) noted, change in the schools continues to be a slow process. But with continued persistence, reforms such as project-based learning and service learning may become part of the mainstream.

REFERENCES

Brookfield, S., & Preskill, S. (1999). *Discussion as a way of teaching*. San Francisco: Jossey-Bass.

Caine, G., & Caine, R. N. (2001). *The brain, education, and the competitive edge*. Lanham, MD: Scarecrow Press.

Dewey, J. (1916). *Democracy and education*. New York: Free Press.

Dewey, J. (1938). *Experience and education*. New York: Free Press.

Dewey, J. (1973). Interest in relation to the training of the will. In J. J. McDermott (Ed.), *The Philosophy of John Dewey*. Chicago: University of Chicago Press.

Gardner, H. (1993). *Frames of mind: The theory of multiple intelligence, 10th anniversary edition*. New York: Basic Books.

Heinecke, W. F., Curry-Corcoran, D. E., & Moon, T. R. (2003). U.S. schools and the new standards and accountability initiative. In D. Duke, M. Grogan, P. Tucker, & W. Heinecke (Eds.), *Educational leadership in an age of accountability*. Albany: State University of New York Press.

Levine, A., & Cureton, J. S. (1998). *When hope and fear collide: A portrait of today's college student*. San Francisco: Jossey-Bass.

Levine, E. (2002). *One kid at a time*. New York: Teachers College Press.

Marzano, R. J. (1992). *A different kind of classroom*. Alexandria, VA: Association for Supervision and Curriculum Development.

McKeachie, W. J. (1999). *Teaching tips: Strategies, research, and theory for college and university teachers*. Lexington, MA: D.C. Heath.

Newell, R. (2003). *Passion for learning: How a project-based system meets the needs of 21st-century students*. Lanham, MD: Scarecrow Press.

Rothman, R. (2001). One hundred fifty years of testing. In *The Jossey Bass Reader on School Reform*. San Francisco: Jossey-Bass.

Wald, P. J., & Castleberry, M. S. (2000). *Educators as learners: Creating professional learning communities*. Alexandria, VA: Association for Supervision and Curriculum Development.

Whitehead, A. N. (1929). *The aims of education*. New York: Free Press.

8

Teaching Excellence through Place-Based Projects

James Lewicki

Just as a pile of stones is not a house, an accumulation of facts and equations is not knowledge.

—Jules Henri Poincare

Aunt Addie Norton said, "I tell you one thing, if you learn it by yourself, if you have to dig for it, it never leaves you. It stays there as long as you live because you had to dig it out of the mud before you learned what it was." Ernest, a sixteen-year-old from Alabama, adds, "Adults may have had a bad experience and they don't want to touch a subject, whereas youth will be ready to go in and dig it up and see what's there." These two quotes give us pause to think about how and what we teach.

Excellence in teaching can take many forms. A time-tested though recently invigorated form is place-based, project-oriented learning. As old as good teaching itself, this pedagogy brings varied subject material, relevant community issues, and a collaborative learning community together to achieve a project goal by "digging" for answers.

Vito Perrone (1991), an exceptional teacher and former dean of the Harvard Graduate School of Education, could speak with force about this type of excellence in teaching. In his *A Letter to Teachers*, he asserts, "The exceptional teachers I know are passionate about learning. They have deep interests in some aspect of learning: history, literature, and science. They are so steeped in this passion that they could manage well if all the textbooks,

workbooks, and curriculum guides that fill the schools suddenly disap-
peared. They see connecting points everywhere" (117).

Greg Wegner, history professor at the University of Wisconsin–LaCrosse,
gave me a gem of a book about teaching, called *Public School Methods*, published in 1922. The introduction had many wonderful statements, and one
caught my eye: "He [the student] must not, because of any scholastic aris-
tocracy on the part of the teacher, be unable to make his contribution to human needs and to know the joy of work well done" (4).

Both the previously mentioned maxim and Perrone's letter provide
bookends, a vision for teaching excellence in place-based, project-oriented
teaching. Whether contributing through work well done or making connections, the unfolding of these complementary principles of place-based
education results in both student-driven and teacher-facilitated projects that
provide powerful learning for both.

Teachers begin to say, "Yes, I can see the importance of that project."
Another teacher proclaims, "What a powerful reason to include projects
in the design of my units." A third teacher may echo, "It would be great
to collaborate with my peers on a project that benefits the community." In
effect, an affirmation is the usual response regarding discussions of place-
based education. Yet a contrary reality exists when it comes to actually
implementing these projects in schools. Teachers may agree, but few step
forward and implement. This dilemma leaves the following question to
pursue: If place-based projects are such powerful pieces of learning, why
don't more teachers subscribe to it in their daily teaching?

Though excellent examples of place-based projects can be found in
schools across America, those examples remain a selective few rather than
a breakthrough in mainstream teaching. The dominant methodology remains fairly consistent these past several generations: teacher locus of control and textbook- and worksheet-driven, pencil-and-paper assignments.
The end result is too frequently a student disconnect, compounded by a
broken-down and ineffective school-to-community linkage.

From the student's point of view, school unfolds with 90 percent of
each day, inside, within the physical structure built to house the learning
at hand. Imagine for a moment the student's realities: waking up each
morning, preparing for school, maybe wondering what the six or seven
teachers have planned for them this particular day, and looking out the
window, noticing the weather, making no connection between the school

day ahead and the weather overhead, unless it's a rare field trip day. As for community, the issues outside of school seldom register on the student's radar screen. Why should they? The difference a student makes is narrowed to the friends and classes they are about to attend, which seldom ask for a community-inspired contribution.

This viewpoint can easily reverse for the teacher. Imagine the teacher driving to work as the student is looking out the bus window. The teacher, though very clear on what will transpire in his or her classroom, seldom knows what the student will be doing in the same building the other 85 percent of the day.

Though learning community is often a spoken goal of schools these days, the school day itself is too often fractured. The unity of time and structure necessary to develop a community of learners is haphazard at best. The nature of our eight-period or four-block system is disjointed, allowing for little communication or shared learning between the silos of being a student or being a teacher. All are housed in a place removed both physically and psychologically from the community. Is it no wonder this state of disconnect works counter to the fundamental purpose for schooling in the first place?

Perrone (1998), in another writing, describes John Dewey's approach to education, which can bridge this disconnect:

> Dewey stressed the need for a new pedagogy that calls upon teachers to integrate the content of schooling with the activities of daily life. He understood the prevailing separation between schooling and life as assuring a limited education for children and young people, emptying the possibilities. In addition he viewed education at its best as growth in understanding, capacity, self-discovery, control of events, and ability to define the world—in other words, as always leading somewhere. (19)

Unless teachers are careful to build a learning community and, more precisely, a community of learners that is "leading somewhere," to counter schools' structural tendencies to fragment learning, we should expect the obvious. Regardless of heroic individual teacher and administrative efforts, schools will be places leading to student alienation.

Place-based education, like other best practices, builds teams of learners. Distinctive to its place-based philosophy, these teams look for ways to make a difference in the community. Dewey believed education was at its best when students learned from the familiar material of ordinary experience. As such, place-based education is not exceptional; rather, it is educating with the "familiar material" of the local community by expanding the range of "ordinary experience." I call this organizing principal "community sensibility," each teacher blending an expert grasp of academic objectives with community awareness as the central feature of the learning at hand. In effect, looking to the community for context, it is relatively easy, as Dewey phrased it, "to put the student in the habitual attitude of finding point of contact and mutual bearings" (Perrone 1998, 19).

Returning to the question raised earlier, why do most teachers fail to adopt this practice? Ron Newell, learning program director at EdVisions, suggests that the traditional pedagogical comfort zone is attractive:

> Moving teachers to a new mode, which means giving up the very reasons they may have liked teaching (control, content, isolation, etc) is asking a great deal—change is always hard. But, if the rewards can be captured as you have mentioned, it makes it all worthwhile. We always say that you don't necessarily work harder, but you will work differently. Finding a comfort zone in the [project-based] work is also very important but not so comfortable that you do not continue to grow. (Newell 2003, 55)

Newell's comment on teaching comfort zones is central to how such a best practice is often agreed to in theory though infrequently put into practice. Veteran teachers, like any professional group, select certain pathways that, year after year, become their dominant manner and style. Third-grade teachers seldom shift to teaching eighth grade, though their certification may allow for that. It takes time to develop both the competencies and confidence as a teacher. We all know the travails of the first-year teacher: much work, much trial and error, and much anxiety. Having once experienced those discomforts, why would a veteran teacher want to shift from an earned comfort zone to one developing place-based projects, where the work seems to constantly reinvent itself, embracing, in a sense, those early teaching challenges?

While facilitating a score of project-based teacher workshops, I listened carefully to my colleagues discuss the hard realities of engaging students in place-based, project-type learning. Four answers seem to resonate during these discussions, and, interestingly enough, these four reasons that a teacher would *practice* this pedagogy are the exact four reasons that a student *values* it. Allow me to start with the student's viewpoint and then transition to the teacher's.

Imagine a student, a teenager these days, full of exuberance, full of life. As a father of five, my son and four daughters have taught me much. Always up front, their smiles of hope and jumps of joy are never far from my experiences of life. Then I drive to school, and what do I see? A significant contrast and, at times, a professional disappointment.

Certainly large numbers of young people enjoy and look forward to their schooling experience. In addition, large numbers of teachers have spent their working lives creating positive classrooms and extracurricular opportunities devoted to the best interests of these students. Numerous classrooms or athletic or performing venues are highly successful. Yet these same dedicated teachers would agree too often that for each student who is engaged, another student is disconnected from the exuberance of learning and participation.

How can this be? As a parent, I empathetically attempt to apply my mind to this conundrum. How can the energy of youth be thwarted to such a degree that significant numbers of disconnected youth remain in every school? I realize the percentages change with each school. But whatever the actual numbers, they represent too many students. Would I accept three of my children being engaged in life and the other two disconnected? Of course not. My measure of success, like yours, is 100 percent. Should we expect the school success rate to be any different?

Look closely at your school: how many students are truly involved in the academic life of your school? How many students are involved in at least one extracurricular activity? In many schools, half involved would be a worthy percentage. Why do I ask about extracurricula? Extracurricular activities, like projects, demand involvement as opposed to participation. Involvement requires a sustained initiative and capacity, whereas participation asks for following directions, response, and, all too often, limited performance.

One spring, during a sixth-grade outdoor education camp, I stayed up late with the senior boy counselors pushing sticks into the dying embers of an evening campfire. It was a reflective moment with several of the most academic and athletically talented students our school had produced. Their comments and reflections made it abundantly clear that they knew how to participate and get the A's for college. They could perform, score well on tests, and ultimately satisfy the adults at school as well as those at home. I found intriguing how the conversation would move to their involvement level. Each young man talked passionately about the football team, acting in the play, playing in the band; these memories held their attention and clearly were the stuff of involvement, where the participation in classes was a distant second.

This campfire experience dovetails with another experience years earlier at a teacher's conference. William Glasser, noted educator, tried to engage a handful of eighth-grade students on the stage before several hundred teachers. His solitary question, "What makes you feel important at school?" received a silent response of bewildered eyes searching for an answer. After a couple of very long minutes, Glasser restated the question. Still no answer. Finally, a student offered, "Is it OK if it is sport?"

"Certainly," replied Glasser. Then the floodgates opened: playing football, volleyball, and the middle school play, organizing dances, cheerleading, on and on. Not a breath of academics. Not even a glimmer of recognition that they, as individual students, may feel important in English, science, math, or social studies.

It is at this juncture that place-based education and its successful projects can make a monumental difference in the way that students are actively involved in school. Not meaning to negate the strong feeling for student involvement in extracurricular activities, it is a positive factor. But there is also value in including this level of engagement in their academic life. A well-run learning community can be like a well-coached team.

Though it had its stories of difficulty, the one-room school mostly shined as a great example of a fully engaged learning community. Ben Logan (1975), reflecting on his education in the Kickapoo Valley of southwestern Wisconsin, writes:

> We didn't know it at the time, but we may have been participants in the best educational system ever devised. In that richly varied one-room community there was no artificial separation of children into good and bad, smart and dumb, young and old. We were all in it together. Subjects and years weren't tied into neat bundles. They all overlapped, so that there was only one subject: education. . . . The process was so natural to me that I took it all for granted. It was like life on the farm, with everything at once, each thing related to everything else. I had trouble later in high school and college. I was

bewildered by the separation of subjects into isolated units, as though chemistry lived on separate planet that didn't even share the same orbit with history. There was no such separation in our one-room community. (36)

The goal of place-based, project-oriented education is to build strong
learning communities. This is evident in the myriad schools that have
adopted project learning. Once it becomes successful, project learning de-
creases the active number of students disengaged and alienated from
school by providing a wide-ranging anchor of purpose for student learning. Teaching with projects looks like Logan's one-room school, unified
under one subject: education.

What are the reasons that teachers and students value project learning?
It serves purpose, makes a difference, is dynamic learning, and enables
belonging. The four, independent of each other, are powerful ingredients
in learning. Together, they are quite a package.

Projects are purposeful. When purpose is real, one feels important because one *is* important. For teenagers, this feeling of worth is critical. This
is also true for teachers as they manage and work with students to complete projects. The authentic audience underscores this purpose for students during the project cycle. And, of course, the community benefit cements this sense of purpose. When my students replanted an entire
downtown park with over 100 trees and shrubs, the visibility reaped benefits for years to come. Many years later, I meet students who remind me
of their sense of accomplishment as they drive by the park.

Projects make a difference. The assorted skills to complete a project
produce clear feedback for both student and teacher. This feedback is real
and often produces unambiguous statements such as "I can do this; I can't
do that; I need help here; I can help someone there; I appreciate others;
others appreciate me; this project helped my community, my school, and
my skills." Like the final score of a game, projects have real outcomes for
the individual and real outcomes for the community. Building a series of
community park benches, creating a historical walking tour brochure, and
helping restore a natural habitat are activities that make a difference.
Nicole, age fifteen, engaged in a project, captured this sense well when
she stated, "I learned more about myself, my peers, and my community
than I could possibly imagine. It is incredible to see so many people with
a strong passion working together to make their dreams happen. I learned

to trust and respect people for the good that they had. It is an incredible feeling to work with people and make a successful product. I did things that I didn't think I could."

This is dynamic learning. The answers aren't always known ahead of time. Sometimes students build the bridge as they walk on it. One piece of learning often leads to a new understanding, which may frame a new inquiry leading to unplanned aspects of the project that will need attention. Frequently a fresh sense of originality exists in a place-based project. And, like any real-life endeavor, there is a constant dynamic of matching the challenge of the project itself with the ability of the group and individuals experiencing the project.

This kind of learning develops belonging. Glasser found that middle school students expressed a sense of belonging when engaged in sports. This sense of belonging occurs in place-based education as well. Implicit in each learning community, when formed around projects, is a vital sense of belonging, courage, and a passion for learning. For teachers, often faced with the social isolation of the classroom, these benefits are reason alone to implement projects. Simply being able to work in tandem with other educators, doing successful projects in collaboration, and working with a team of teachers and a dynamic group of students is an experience worth the challenge inherent in changing instructional pedagogy. In addition, experiencing the impact in the community revitalizes the school itself and cements this change.

Education based on projects in the community is nothing new. It would be valuable to examine, for a moment, the richness found in generations of teachers who have successfully used this approach. Place-based education and its theoretical base, constructivist learning theory, embrace the understanding that for generations community experiences were the stuff of good teaching. And where you have solid learning in close school–community connections, you have place-based education.

There exists a medley of constructivist sentiments written by educators over the years, echoing place-based instructional insights right to this day. Whether in 1922 or today, educators have a very accessible archive of successful teaching to guide us in our work. Books regarding teaching and education written before World War II are treasure troves of guidance, general and specific, for place-based educators. Written at a time when the barriers between the professionalism of education and the purpose of schooling in the community were more permeable, these books contain numerous examples of projects and programs that powerfully engaged students in their community. The details given to some of these lessons, where there is a natural integration of science with the humanities, is really inspiring:

> With most education still in rural communities, and most teachers still in the role of generalist, it was expected that teachers taught across the curriculum. It was the norm to find the English teacher two periods later conducting a field walk in the neighboring forest pointing out the spring flora; it was the norm to find the agriculture teacher partnering with area farmers to repair local machinery, then in the afternoon connect the morning activity with the afternoon lesson in the classroom; and it was the norm to find the history teacher also the president of the local historical society. Besides this diverse teaching portfolio that kept teachers teaching as generalists, instruction was augmented by a flow of elders into the school and conversely, students flowing into the community listening to the sharing of stories, building a legacy.

The philosophy of constructivism was inherent in these works. "Each quest opens many new lines of thought; interest deepens as the list of discovering lengthens," wrote the authors of volume 2 of *Public School Methods* (1992, 2). This seven-volume work extensively examined the entire K–12 curriculum in both broad philosophical strokes as well as minute, helpful detail. Like a teacher's Sears Roebuck catalog, it might be the one set of books a rural teacher could employ to run a small school:

> Pages were even full of detailed projects like robin studies, grapevine orchards, how to build a terrarium, and lessons on the common housefly. There was a project-based calendar, tied to the seasons for each week of the year! Understanding of deep, comprehensive projects was evident as well. For example, a study of a brook was conceived as a place study for an entire year.

Alfred North Whitehead (1958) spoke of the danger of "inert ideas, that is to say, ideas that are merely received into the mind without being utilized or tested or thrown into fresh combinations" (115). In fact, Whitehead went on to declare that, "education with inert ideas is not only useless; it is, above all things, harmful" (115). Knowledge being tested, utilized, and thrown into fresh combinations is another way to define place-based learning.

Continuing historical reading, I discovered a wonderful document by Sir John Livingston titled *Education for a World Adrift* (1944). Written during a summer of war, this was a significant work to guide the British government as it reorganized the school system to meet a looming post-war demand to extend equality to all. Livingston writes, "The test of a successful education is not the amount of knowledge that a pupil takes away from school, but his appetite to know and his capacity to learn" (28). This capacity to learn is what Vito Perrone pointed out, what Ben Logan spoke of, and what moves a teacher to adopt place-based, project-oriented learning.

But exactly what are these fundamental capacities, beyond a subject area expertise, that support a teacher's shift into this teaching pedagogy? Ted Sizer uttered a memorable quote in *Horace's Compromise: The Dilemmas of the American High School* (1984): "The people are better than the structure. Therefore, the structure must be at fault" (209). I could not agree more. The teachers I know are dedicated folks who give many unheralded moments to young people. Some schools have great leadership, some have dismal leadership. Nevertheless, teachers forge ahead, regardless, with personal visions that speak volumes.

Since the teacher–student relationship is central to the learning in projects, finding a teacher is a critical step. What does it take to teach in a project-based school? What does a commitment to place-based projects ask of the teacher, and what characteristics are embodied? William Glasser (1986) noted how "life in school must be thought of as life itself, not simply preparation for later life. Life in school—for adults as well as for children—must be lived fully. And again, in a democracy, school life should embody democratic (rather than say, authoritarian, autocratic, bureaucratic, or feudal) principles" (83). Glasser clearly felt that the way for small learning teams in schools to succeed was to "redistribute the power to get more productivity" (83) This is also true of teacher characteristics; being open to something new and dynamic is a necessary mind-set for teachers of project learning.

Teachers being open to a fresh approach was the view of students as well. Although only fourteen years old, Kelly, Chris, and Ximena, students I taught through place-based project learning, spoke eloquently. Kelly underscores the above statements when she said, "Learning is asking questions and finding answers. It's discovering things about the world and your past that you never knew. Learning can introduce all kinds of new ideas. It can make you wonder, Why? And how? Instead of taking things for granted." Of course, she nails the critical feature: not taking things for granted. What a great trait for project learners, expecting the unexpected.

Chris adds the social dimension of learning when he asserts, "Learning can happen in many different ways. Sometimes a learning community must learn from each other." This interdependence in a project allows the students to meet the unexpected with confidence.

And then Ximena joins in with what she believes: "Learning is gaining knowledge. Learning does not have to take place in school, you can learn from just about everything in life. I think that sometimes the things you decide to learn on your own will stick with you all your life."

Teaching with this kind of student authenticity is doubly rewarding because, like a fire, projects kindle the greatness in teachers as well. William Ayers (1993), noted Chicago educator, discussed this greatness in teaching. Though I usually shy away from long extended quotes, I feel this one merits the depth:

> Greatness in teaching also requires getting over the notion that teaching is a set of techniques or disconnected methods. There are lots of people who write adequate lesson plans, or keep order and quiet in their classrooms, and deliver competent instruction in algebra or phonics . . . outstanding teachers engage youngsters, interact with them, draw energy and direction from them, and find ways to give them a reason to follow along. This is the difficult and serious work of teaching. Greatness in teaching, as in acting or writing, is always in pursuit of the next utterance, the next performance, and the next encounter. It is not—can never be—finished or summed up . . . great teaching demands an openness to something new, something unique, and something dynamic. In teaching it must always be, "here we go again." (129)

In order to enlarge the dynamic of learning, the challenge for teachers is to cocreate these opportunities with the students that will enable growth and development into more self-initiated projects that eventually lead to student control of learning. Ayers continues, "We know we are successful when students are willing to forge their own next steps, when they face the future with some love, some indignation, and a lot of courage" (137).

These kinds of teachers are not rare. Many of our colleagues would love this opportunity. Since place-based learning is very much a continuous means of connecting people, resources, and meaningfulness together, it is imperative to find teachers with an "action bias" toward this kind of facilitative teaching. This facilitative effort requires each teacher to analyze the learning exhibited in various projects and draw out the enduring knowledge. Knowledge of skills such as scientific investigation, teamwork capability, presentation styles, analysis of data, and writing press releases are a few examples.

What does it take? In my experience as a place-based teacher and leader of workshops for others who need support in this endeavor, I am convinced that the following three basic capacities must be present for success: a proven aptitude for lifelong learning, unconditional regard for the success of each student, and an ability to communicate and build rapport in multiple surroundings with a wide variety of people.

We use the term "lifelong learning skills" often but seldom pause to examine its precise list of skills. What does it really mean to have these skills? Certainly, someone who loves to gather new information, solve problems, and make connections is a place to start, but let's not end there. The Illinois Math and Science Academy faculty suggests a list that I have adapted to guide others in curriculum work:

- Develop the intellectual habit of skepticism and openness
- Demonstrate a recognition and utilization of dynamic systems and structures
- Develop the power of intuition
- Develop mathematical relationships based on empirical data involving multiple variables
- Demonstrate effective collaboration skills, in the pursuit of questions that are pertinent, insightful, and reveal deep understanding
- Exhibit tenacity as a learner
- Precisely observe, record, and analyze data, always evaluating appropriateness, reliability, and validity
- Utilize the discipline of deduction
- Demonstrate the ability to cooperate through a shared dilemma
- Select problem-solving processes appropriate to a problem
- Recognize, allow, and seek alternative problem-solving strategies

- Draw conclusions independently of authority
- Tolerate ambiguity — and the potential for more than one correct answer

An unconditional regard for the student means putting the student needs ahead of competing adult issues and developing the productive teacher–student relationship. In the end, the quality of relationships is the critical leverage feature in school improvement. John Maguire, Claremont College president, echoed this sentiment in a 1992 report, declaring, "If the relationships are wrong between teachers and students, for whatever reason, you can restructure until the cows come home, but transformation won't take place" (2003, 106).

Projects take us deep into the workings of our communities. Teachers strip away the isolation of the classroom and fundamentally alter their approach to teaching. The best project teachers have an uncanny ability to communicate effectively in multiple surroundings with a wide variety of people. Thomas Sergiovanni (1999) encouraged this view of schooling when he wrote, "If we view schools as communities rather than organizations, the practices that make sense in schools understood as organizations just don't fit. The bonding together of people in special ways and binding of them to shared values and ideas are the defining characteristics of schools as communities" (13). A collaborative and decision-making capacity is essential for a project-based teaching position. The ability to facilitate this development in the students is equally critical.

Having explored the capacities needed for project teaching, how can we guide the shift of teachers from delivery pedagogy to project-based learning? A meaningful approach in an existing school is to break the modality of "business as usual" and work briefly on a project as a teaching team. An isolated, successful miniproject demonstrates the power, passions, and potential of project learning connected to the community. Once teachers experience success, an "action bias" is created that can be nurtured.

One spring, for instance, my colleagues and I obtained a $1,000 grant and created an oral history day. We secured substitutes for ten junior high teachers, allowing staff to spend the day on the project. Each teacher was assigned four students, and as a group visited with and interviewed World War II veterans in their homes. It was terrific to watch the students interview the veterans. One gentleman, a veteran of the 8th Air Force stationed in England, shared stories in the farmhouse kitchen where he was raised. At one point he jumped up and opened an overstuffed drawer. He pulled out his original flight log from 1944. Watching his fingers slide over the tattered book as he recalled various missions was a thrilling moment.

There seems to be a "believability quotient" for experienced teachers to overcome. Does this project learning really work? But once the teachers came back with tales of thrilling learning moments during these oral interviews, it wasn't very difficult to begin conversation around other project scenarios that might fit the existing school structure. We even began conversation around shifting the existing school structure to fit project needs. Either way, a series of short-term, highly visible, and successful projects achieve a momentum that often diminishes the doubters.

As you move forward in place-based teaching, you must give regard to the aspects of power and control, which, if anticipated well, will allow for a smooth, productive learning shift. In many ways, traditional textbook teaching is set up as each teacher having *power over* the student, whereas, in sharp contrast, the typical project is best done with each teacher sharing *power with* the student. *Power with* allows growth and potency; in contrast, *power over*, though more easily managed, restricts growth and potency.

Borrowing from science for a metaphor, the power of a neutron lies in its capacity to be open to the inevitable charter, open to the messages traveling through the larger body. This is an open system. Open systems, by definition, model a *power with* strategy. The power of place-based projects springs from the capacity to be open to the learning at hand and to have each member of the learning community work with each other. When students succeed, there is a surge of attention, excitement, and interest. This comes from sharing the power, not hording it. I tend to agree with Glasser (1986) when he states, "It is this lack of access to power in the academic classes that is so frustrating to students because it comes just at the time when students are beginning to experience the increased need for power which is part of the normal biology of adolescence" (84). *Power with* is a learning multiplier; *power over* is a box with intrinsic limits—it seldom soars.

If you were to decide to start developing some significant projects with your students or decided to take a job in a new innovative or charter project-based school, you would need to keep in mind communication, leadership initiative, responsibility, and core academics. Seldom does a teacher release the thinking of why a certain lesson or unit is undertaken before they teach, whereas in place-based learning, seldom should a project be undertaken without a thorough vetting of the project before it begins. When students, teachers, and community members discuss the merits of the project, they then sign off on its worthiness and build a rationale for its merits. This process, of course, takes clear communication, respect, and courtesy.

Developing leadership with students is a stair-step proposition, sequential and incremental. Design good leadership experiences based from the needs of the project early in the process. Manage this leadership so that no one is overwhelmed and make sure there is fair distribution of real leadership. For example, one student might be assigned research, another communication, yet another graphics. Create leadership teams. And, finally, always be ready to give away some of the teacher power. Why? Because you understand that it leverages much more learning than you could ever create alone.

Too often student responsibility atrophies by middle school. Students are veterans of having their responsibility narrowed to the lesson–assignment–test cycle. Usually projects are controlled by the teacher with specific tasks he or she has designed to complete each project. Students merely follow along a prescribed path. The kind of project-based learning that we have explored in these pages is one where the student role is consciously upgraded at every opportunity. Lifelong learning skills are attained by full involvement and shared responsibility. As you work with projects, remember the four kinds of responsibilities: self-responsibility, responsibility to others, responsibility to the community, and responsibility to the learning.

Place-based learning contrasts with traditional pedagogies in that students possess a strong bias for independent learning. The focus and motivation are there in projects, and the applications reduce the inconsequential moments of the school experience. The results are reinvigorated, connected, and productive learning times. As this energy is increased, keep in mind the basic academics. It's great that advanced understanding takes place, and many highly visible moments will tell many an enriching story—but when the project is complete, it is only fair for each parent to ask if their son and/or daughter's reading, writing, and mathematical capacities are better.

Working with over 100 project teachers this past year, the most consistent sentiment I heard was to embed the basic skills in these projects as well.

Finally, in place-based projects, students make lifelong connections because of their sense of accomplishment and sense of belonging to something achieved greater than themselves. Science, again, provides a model, for we know that life is created and sustained by deep interconnections. Where we once saw separate entities, we now understand flows and currents of energy, matter, and information. From atoms and cells to plants and society, dynamic patterns operate with open systems. Whether science or projects, the organizing principle is the same: making connections. As Dean Lind (2003), a Minnesota New Country School teacher explains, "How far could you get from natural learning than to teach disconnected subjects out of context? Would you teach someone how to build a house by teaching a class on pounding nails, cutting lumber, and putting on shingles—then later build the house? I believe learning is in a large sense connecting, putting information together. That sure is contrary to the 'pulling apart' that is done in a traditional school" (42).

What is this sense of belonging? To be part of something more than you, to be part of a team, thereby influencing others and making a difference. This sense of belonging is vital for teachers as well as students. In these active schools of hundreds of students, classroom teaching can be a lonely occupation, whereas projects, with multiple alliances between school adults and community adults, lead to a growth in a teacher's sense of belonging. For my colleagues, this benefit easily makes up for the extra time in this renewed teaching challenge, where the answers are not always a file cabinet away.

Recently I met with a dozen educators interested in developing projects with their students. A question was raised regarding creating interest on the part of other teachers. My answer was that no matter how creative, each classroom teacher reaches their limit of capacity and power. In contrast, a project team expands this level of creativity and power, leveraging a whole new array of learning possibilities. As Michael Fullan (1993) explains, "You cannot have students as continuous learners and effective collaborators, without teachers having the same characteristics" (46). Being able to run a local newspaper, change a zoning law, develop a business, conduct original research, and shape an art foundation's goals are worthy and significant efforts, complex by their very nature. This exponential surge of capacity and power, in service to others, is the single biggest draw to place-based, project-oriented learning. Teaching is touching the future. And it is wonderful to hear from our students who have participated over the years. My students always vividly recall their projects.

Project teaching warrants a thoughtful approach. I trust that this discussion has illuminated, from my experience and the quotes from others, this thoughtfulness. Significant learning itself, which permeates projects, has been my passion for years. By creating projects with your students, you will acquire the firsthand knowledge to achieve and believe in significant learning opportunities that produce knowledge. As Sergiovanni (1999) explained, "Instead of being dispensers of knowledge, teachers — like physicians, lawyers, architects, and other professionals — must become producers of knowledge. Professionals transmit and dispense, but at root their job is to produce something worth transmitting or dispensing in the first place. Professionals create knowledge in use as they practice" (4).

REFERENCES

Ayers, W. (1993). *To teach: The journey of a teacher*. New York: Teachers College Press.

Fullan, M. (1993). *Change forces: Probing the depth of educational reform*. London: Falmer Press.

Glasser, W. (1986). *Control theory in the classroom*. New York: Harper & Row.

Lind, D. (2003). *EdVisions forum discussion*. Posting no. 42 of 150, http://www.edvisions.coop (accessed January 30, 2003).

Livingston, J. (1944). *Education for a world adrift*. London: Macmillan.

Logan, B. (1975). *The land remembers*. New York: Viking.

Maguire, J. (1992). *Report to the institute for education and transformation*. Claremont, CA: Claremont Graduate School. As quoted by Andrea Martin in the EdVisions forum discussion, posting no. 106 of 150, http://www.edvisions.coop (accessed February 6, 2003).

Newell, R. (2003). *EdVisions forum discussion*. Posting no. 55 of 150, http://www.edvisions.coop (accessed January 30, 2003).

Perrone, V. (1991). *A letter to teachers: Reflections on schooling and the art of teaching*. San Francisco: Jossey-Bass.

Perrone, V. (1998). Why do we need a pedagogy of understanding? In Martha Stone Wiske (Ed.), *Teaching for understanding: Linking research with practice*. San Francisco: Jossey-Bass.

Public school methods, Vol. 2. (1922). Chicago: School Methods Publishing Co.

Sergiovanni, T. (1999). *Building community in schools*. San Francisco: Jossey-Bass.

Sizer, T. (1984). *Horace's compromise: The dilemma of the American high school*. New York: Houghton Mifflin.

Whitehead, A. N. (1958). *The aims of education*. New York: Macmillan.

Part 3

SOME RESULTS OF THE LEARNING COMMUNITIES

Following are three chapters that give a flavor of what it means to have been a part of an EdVisions Learning Community. From these few results, the reader can see that great things are happening or can happen. From these results we know that we can change everything!

9

MNCS Graduates: Telling Lived Stories

Vivian Johnson, Peg Lonnquist, and Walter Enloe

Minnesota New Country School (MNCS) graduates tell stories offering both wild support and insightful critiques of their school. It is clear that MNCS graduates loved the opportunity to pursue their own interests, be challenged, and not feel that they were wasting their time. Selected quotes from a 2002 survey of graduates (who have been given different pseudonyms) document the difference between the MNCS experience and that of traditional schools:

> When I was in [traditional] school and when I was home schooled it was more of a book learning. I think the thing I really learned from MNCS was that that is not the *only* way you can learn, there's tons of different ways. That's what I really liked (Jamie).

> Minnesota New Country School changed my life. I learned so much more about life and about myself than I would have at a traditional high school . . . they encouraged me from eighth grade to study and research professions that interested me. So that's what I spent most of my time doing. It allowed me to completely realize my passion (John).

> I liked that advisers are not there to spoon feed you. Their role is more of supporting you in taking initiative, how to do research. Most kids are spoon fed by teachers so they don't really grow intellectually (Marisa).

> You are free to choose. And the freedom that you could say that you didn't like something and they were pretty much open to change (Jamie).

My adviser used to take me with him to state capitol meetings with politicians and committees. I just learned by being there. I know I can do almost anything (Marisa).

As a result of attending MNCS, I'm involved in local politics, I'm active as a citizen, I vote, and I get involved in campaigns. And I get other people involved. Someday I will run for office (Cecilia).

On the other hand, being enthusiastic about the MNCS experience did not inhibit supportive graduates such as Meredith and Sarah, from offering insightful critiques and suggestions for school improvement:

MNCS has a good idea and good plans for learning, but has problems with staff understanding and following through with these goals. I had the best adviser I could ever ask for, but unfortunately other students weren't so lucky . . . MNCS needs to really evaluate their staff and ways of implementing the learning goals they had set up eight years ago (Meredith).

If you're not [self-motivated] you are expected to be that way to leave there with a diploma. It is not like a regular school that you go there and classes are waiting for you all day. You must be able to think of your own work and complete it (Sarah).

THE STUDY BEGINS

Nine years after opening MNCS, advisers knew in their hearts that powerful, authentic learning had occurred repeatedly as a result of the schools project-based approach to learning. Their intuition was supported by surveys (Thomas et al. 2001) summarizing that MNCS students compared favorably with their peers on the Minnesota Basic Standards Tests (math, reading, and writing) and outscored them on language measures. In addition, Tom Vander Ark of the Gates Foundation wrote the following to the MNCS advisers: "We have scoured the country to find people like you, people who have taken this belief and successfully created a teaching and learning environment that fosters high achievement by all. . . . The Minnesota New Country School is the coolest school in America."

However, these MNCS advisers were interested in systematically documenting the impact of the MNCS experience and enlisted our help in developing a research protocol.

As teachers in the Graduate School of Education at Hamline University, we saw our role as devising a process where the MNCS advisers could identify the primary areas needing exploration with their graduates and conducting the survey and semistructured interviews. (Survey protocol can be obtained by e-mailing the authors at vjohnson@hamline.edu.) During a series of meetings, MNCS advisers narrowed their questions to the following five areas:

- Project-based skills
- Individual responsibility
- Resilience/persistence skills
- Reflection skills
- Relationship skills

MNCS graduates' perceptions of their experiences in these five areas, as well as some additional benefits and recommendations that they highlighted, are reflected in this study. To provide context for their stories, we begin with a description of the learning environment in this unique school.

A DIFFERENT ENVIRONMENT WHERE LEARNING IS RELEVANT

The initial observation when entering MNCS is a large open area filled with large tables, surrounded on three sides by small computer workstations and on the fourth side a small stage. Adjoining rooms include a media center, a craft room, a science lab area, a small stage, and an atrium. Teens and adults are found in pairs or alone engaged in myriad activities. One learner is working alone on a computer finishing a project on robotics. Three or four others are discussing what they learned about carding wool at a local Angora goat farm. Several more are socializing or playing chess. Others are consulting with their adviser. Leaving the large open area and going into an adjacent room, the visitor observes another learner explaining his two-year study of the Minnesota River's pH levels to a younger student. While listening to the conversation, it becomes clear that the younger student is going to continue the study after the older one graduates. Other students are off campus taking advanced placement courses, consulting with experts in their field of study, or building a boat.

For the prospective student, perhaps the biggest surprise is the role of the MNCS teachers. The teachers (called "advisers" to more accurately reflect their role) guide students in locating resources and fine-tuning the goals of their projects. The occasional foray into the traditional teacher role might include teaching photography resulting in student photo essays, leading an environmental education bike trip, conducting an archaeological dig, directing a play, or assisting with fund-raising and supervising a study trip on geology and culture to Hawaii. All of this is possible because MNCS strives for "a different environment so that learning is relevant and interesting" (Marisa). As the description unfolds, it is clear that this "different environment" at MNCS is based on project-based learning.

MNCS founders chose project-based learning because they believe it is more aligned with the world students will encounter after graduation. Project-based learning requires that students choose, plan, research, and complete standards-based projects, many of which result in real-life products. Working on the projects requires creativity, problem-solving, teamwork, time management, communication, and assessment. With multiple opportunities to engage in project-based learning, students strengthen skills that advisers believe are essential for success. Graduates agree. As one former student wrote, "At MNCS, I was allowed and encouraged to use my own creativity in my work and my personal intellect was respected. In this way, MNCS prepared me well for college." While project-based learning fosters learner independence, it does not allow free reign, as some people perceive.

At MNCS, students have a great deal of latitude to follow their own interests. However, the process of following one's specific interest must also support the development of competencies described in the Minnesota Graduation Standards. Furthermore, all projects must be presented before three adults (two advisers and another adult) for approval. The learner must be able to articulate a project's rationale and how its pursuit will make them a better person in five years.

Once approved, the advisers and parents provide encouragement, but the students themselves are responsible for reporting their use of time and for initiating, completing, and presenting their final projects. Sarah sums up project-based learning at MNCS: "It is not like a regular school that you go there and classes are waiting for you all day. You must be able to think of your own work and complete it." Throughout the study, Sarah and other graduates provided us with a rich sense of the impact the MNCS experience had on the developing of project-based skills, individual responsibility, resilience/persistence, reflection, and relationship skills, the five areas of most interest to MNCS advisers.

PROJECT-BASED SKILLS

No classrooms, no bells, no teachers standing in front of a class, yet many of MNCS graduates participating in this study describe deep learning from their remarkable projects. As Cecelia explains, she enjoyed balancing several projects at once. "[I am] most proud of the yearbook and my senior project which studied twenty-one schools and the effects of barometric pressure on student behavior . . . I started college [PSEO] after six months at MNCS . . . I had the top state project in the science fair and was first alternate to the International Science Fair." As a future scientist, Beth explained that project-based learning coupled with a supportive adviser allowed her to explore her passions. "My absolute favorite project was my senior project, I wish I were still in high school to continue doing it. . . . My senior project was on hypoxia in the Dead Zone in the Gulf of Mexico and I was tracing that all the way back to Sibley County because I wanted to relate this huge environmental problem to the people in the little-bitty county on the Mississippi River."

A number of projects each year must be completed individually and others with a team so that students develop both skills. One group of MNCS students created a computerized embroidery design business and "learned everything from beginning to end to start a business" (Cecelia). As she describes the process, the number of higher-order thinking skills required to complete a complex project become clear. In this case, the learners first developed the business concept. Then they wrote a business plan and revised it several times. The design business also required students to investigate machines and equipment needed, apply for a business license and business loans, attend IRS training seminars on taxes and accounting, and then market their product. Finally, these students developed invoices, kept sales and purchase journals, and filed tax returns. The profits either returned to the business or were given as postsecondary scholarships to the students involved. Several students have continued the business after the founders graduated. One member of this team started her own business while at MNCS and now operates it full time. "I had to learn how to create a business legally. So I had to correspond and do all the work with Minnesota's Secretary of State Office" (Marissa). Other graduates also describe noteworthy projects of their own or their peers.

For example, Kent researched and built a straw bale structure. Jennifer conducted an experiential analysis of teen behavior toward impoverished peers. Art researched tigers as an endangered species. Lynette created a historical time line of events that had a profound impact on the world. Susan wrote a paper on the history of quilting in the United States. A group project led to students monitoring the deformed frogs discovered in a pond located near the school.

INDIVIDUAL RESPONSIBILITY

The MNCS grads in this study described long-term benefits as a result of having responsibility for their own learning. During an interview, Jamie describes how project-based learning contributed to her evolving understanding of a deadline, maturing as a learner, and the impact of the two on her college experience. According to Jamie:

> When I got to MNCS I didn't have any clue [about deadlines], so then someone had to kind of teach me. Like okay, when about do you want to get this done? . . . then I would set up my own. . . . The advantages in college are that if they tell you to do a paper it doesn't take me long to figure out what I am going to do. I know the process of setting up what to do. Many people have too big of [*sic*] an idea and will never be able to fit it all into a paper. Just research I'm good at. I am also good at setting up my deadlines.

Another student expressed the benefits this way: "I've found the most important skills I've carried with me are not facts and dates, but the ability to draw connections, problem solve, hold myself accountable, and communicate effectively." Marisa concurs. "I think all the independence, and hanging it all on yourself makes, I just like the person I became from it all." Anthony noticed that the other students in his current college courses struggle with learning on their own without teacher direction. In contrast, MNCS "taught independence in learning. What I wanted to learn I could go out and learn, I don't need to find a teacher to go and teach me. I have the independence to know what I want to learn . . . and I took the initiative."

On the other hand, several graduates in our study felt that new students should be given more guidance regarding deadlines: "The only drawback to my education at MNCS was the lack of set deadlines for projects. I think that the students need to be pushed harder to accomplish their goals. The first year of college was difficult for me in sticking to and managing deadlines set by professors, as I was not used to taking deadlines very seriously." "MNCS was a great school to teach a person responsibility; however, if a person is not motivated by learning, there is a bit of room for procrastination." Most of the study participants told us that completing complex projects gave them more opportunity to develop these skills than in a traditional school. However, additional scaffolding by advisers would allow more MNCS learners to obtain the benefits described in this section.

Anthony noticed that his sense of responsibility toward school and his peers was allowed to be expressed in a way that may not have occurred in a traditional school. On occasions when he felt that his friends were not getting the credits they deserved for their projects, he sought out their advisers and argued in their defense. "I felt very strongly about trying to help my friends to make the school a little bit better place for them . . . by the time I left there I was pretty good at getting stuff negotiated."

An understanding of responsibility for their own learning could also be seen in the graduate's description of the role of the adviser. The advisers' responsibility is "supporting you in taking initiative, how to do research . . . [advisers] are not there to spoon feed you" (Marisa).

RESILIENCE/PERSISTENCE SKILLS

Our data indicated that these MNCS graduates were able to research independently and were persistent about finding other solutions when the first approach did not succeed. For example, when a group of students was starting a business, the loan application was denied. Marisa explains that you have to "try again when small business associations or banks refuse you. It's about self-initiative and not giving up."

All the graduates we interviewed indicated that they were already persistent when they came to MNCS but on reflection discovered that they had been granted more opportunity to practice this skill than they would have had at a traditional school. Jamie explained that the opportunity to use this skill is what had attracted her to the school. "To succeed in a place like this, you need to be persistent, you need to be working all the time . . . that's probably the thing about [traditional] school I didn't like was that it was just so boring, you just had to do what the teacher said."

In fact, graduates concurred that students who were not already persistent or able to develop the quality of persistence would not be able to succeed in a project-based learning environment. "If you're not [self-motivated and persistent] you are expected to be that way to leave there with a diploma" (Sarah). However, there is room to develop persistence. Anthony describes struggling with completing projects "basically the whole time I was there . . . I never really wanted to just buck up and finish [a project], I always wanted to start something else before I finished something else" and yet several complex projects were completed by this student.

REFLECTION SKILLS

Students at MNCS were required to reflect on what they learned as part of their assessment as they completed each project. Written and/or verbal reflections were delivered to three adults as well as occasionally to the entire school, parents/guardians, and the community on quarterly "Presentation Nights." Our interviewees often did not expand much on reflection, and we were not clear whether that was because of the phrasing of the question or because it seemed so second nature to them to reflect continually.

In fact, a common response when we asked students about reflection was not about their work but their reflection on the pain of their school's stigma as being a place for slackers. Dealing with this stigma, they felt, caused them to be reflective regarding the need to believe in oneself and the need to turn difficulties into positive learning experiences. One graduate sums up the lesson: "You have to have a thick skin in business and I learned that at school because the town didn't support the school" (Cecelia). Another graduate recalls that the name-calling was hurtful but that "now when my professors ask where I went to school, they are absolutely enthralled with it. They just think that it is so cool" (Marisa).

A unique perspective on reflection at MNCS was expressed by Anthony. "I'm sure it [reflection] helped, but I got really good at playing the system . . . if you can go in there, sit down and answer all their questions, and if you understand it inside and out, you get more credit. I got a lot better at it!" From our perspective, Anthony "got better at" reflection.

RELATIONSHIP SKILLS

MNCS advisers were also interested in the graduates' reflections concerning their ability to deepen relationships with adults and peers. Without a doubt, the first student–adult relationship the students considered, with the advisers, evoked strong feelings—primarily of gratitude and affinity. The view Jamie expressed was frequently stated during our interviews:

> Relationships [with adults at MNCS] are totally different. You know you had to do what they say, but there is something else there, they really care about you and you can tell that. And they really want you to succeed, they really want you to learn . . . and they become more of a friend, friend–adviser. . . . [At the traditional school] I never ever got any feelings like they wanted to help you learn.

Marisa observed that the organizational structure at MNCS, including having the same adviser every year, facilitated the development of deeper relationships with advisers. "We had coffee every morning, students and advisers, talking, connecting. . . . My adviser expected me to lead the first day and I did. That was [another adviser's] attitude too." But just as some of the participants in this study described the positive impact of their relationship with their advisers, others were neutral or negative.

Graduates were distressed about their peers who had advisers who seemed controlling or laissez-faire and thus not as helpful. "One adviser type wants to direct you and directly teach you and hold you in tight control. Others let you do whatever even messing around for months, even years until you decide to get going. The ideal is in the middle. She knows when to kick butt and when to back off. She knows when to push gently knowing the kid will do it eventually" (Cecilia).

After describing close relationships with advisers, graduates cited peer relations as an important aspect of the MNCS experience. Cecelia sums up the general consensus: "I love the camaraderie of the people. . . . I'm still in contact with 90 percent of the people back then, even the ones that dropped out." Beyond the typical social aspect of friendships, we heard about the importance of peers helping each other during the learning process. Jamie describes it this way: "We were friends but we helped each other with our learning too . . . we can have group projects, so that's one way we can help each other learn. Or like at math, towards the end we would all sit at a table, so we can help the younger ones."

Questions regarding the effect on relationships with parents resulted in quite varied responses. Some graduates reported no effect because they already had a close relationship with their parents. A few noted that they probably talked to their parents more about school than they would have had they attended a traditional school and felt proud when their parents attended presentation night. One graduate felt attending MNCS resulted in a strained relationship with her parents because she was so involved in her projects. "My parents did not like the fact that I wanted to go to school all summer long and that I didn't want to be at home, and when I was at home I was reading or working on stuff all the time. . . . My dad was really worried whether I would fit into college or not. . . . My dad was worried that I wasn't taking extracurricular activities like band and stuff like that because it looks good on college applications" (Marisa). Now that she is in college and everything is going well, Marisa's relationship with her parents has improved.

Graduates also reported that their relationship skills were positively impacted by the requirement to work with community experts. "My community expert was wonderful. She helped me get on that river trip. I could call on her. She would call and invite me to things . . . and this was her daily work, it is so thrilling" (Beth). Marisa describes how her experiences with the community experts enhanced her ability to successfully enter the public service area: "I am going to get into politics in the future . . . you know, connections are everything." Working with adults became a norm for MNCS students to a degree that is rare in a traditional school setting. As a result, we noticed that the MNCS grads seemed to lack the inhibition that many teens have when communicating with adults, both in their interactions with us and in their descriptions of past and current interactions.

ADDITIONAL BENEFITS NOTED BY THE GRADUATES

The MNCS students interviewed were perceptive as they reflected on their experiences at the school. All of them responded positively to having attended MNCS and could articulate a depth of learning rarely seen in traditional public schools. During the surveys and interviews, while the MNCS graduates were expressing their ideas about the five areas the advisers had asked us to focus on (project learning, individual responsibility, resilience/ persistence, reflection, and relationship skills), the students identified additional benefits and offered insightful suggestions for improving the environment for future students. The most often identified additional benefits included the following (supporting quotes found earlier in the chapter):

- The freedom to choose their own topics of study (within the Minnesota Graduation Standards framework) and thus take increased interest in their schoolwork
- Encouragement to pursue areas of interest that directed them toward discovery or discard of a career path
- The experience of working in a community of teens and adults that contributed to reciprocal learning

RESEARCHER-IDENTIFIED BENEFITS

Although the graduates were articulate about their learning outcomes, we noted their inability to identify the acquisition of some skills that were readily apparent to the researchers. The most striking was their leadership skills. MNCS holds monthly all-school meetings, and unlike traditional schools, students take part in many decisions that affect the entire school. Individually, students practice leadership by being required to articulate and justify their project ideas. In addition, several students explained how they prepared for and brought unsolicited school improvement ideas to the advisers. One student explained how he advocated for some of his peers when project ideas were not approved because of an adviser's more traditional perspectives on learning. In our experience, this type of student advocacy does not occur in a traditional school. In fact, a student advocating for a peer in this manner may be in trouble with a teacher or principal in a traditional school.

RECOMMENDATIONS FROM THE GRADUATES

Graduates offered five main recommendations for improving their school; the first three relate to the adviser's role and the others to further skill development. The graduates recommended that MNCS do the following:

1. Develop a selection process for advisers and for ongoing professional development so that all advisers follow through with the original philosophy: Graduates described adviser philosophies that ran the spectrum from a completely hands-off approach to one whose approach was much like a traditional teacher's role. The graduates believe that it would increase the success rate of MNCS learners if the advisers define their role and actions more clearly and agree to a common approach that lands somewhere in the middle of these two extremes:

> MNCS has a good idea and good plans for learning, but has problems with staff understanding and following through with these goals. I had the best adviser I could ever ask for, but unfortunately other students weren't so lucky . . . MNCS needs to really evaluate their staff and ways of implementing the learning goals they had set up. (Meredith)

2. Increase training of advisers to assist new students with project completion skills: Graduates in this study concurred that for independent and focused students, this school approaches perfection. They were able to work at their own pace, explore new interests, and discover their strengths. However, for students who are less self-motivated, they observed that only a few of them truly succeeded in finding their passion and flourishing at MNCS. In their opinion, some students might have succeeded had they had more training on project completion skills.

3. Require advisers to participate in more community building, both as role models and for the benefits: Another interesting insight addressed community building. These graduates believed that being part of a "community of learners" was an integral part of the MNCS mission and was a

reality they experienced and appreciated among their peers. However, former students observed that the staff no longer modeled a similar community of learners, to everyone's detriment. "Adults need to take time for themselves and to be a professional community—just like they expect of the students" (Marisa).

4. Counsel students to transfer to another school if project-based learning does not work with their learning style: Graduates concluded that advisers needed to be more proactive with learners who were not experiencing success. They felt it did not help the school's reputation or atmosphere to have students who were not able to work on projects independently and showed no signs of learning that skill. "My brother went [to MNCS] . . . for two years but he failed miserably and got at least a year behind. He was not reaching his potential. He didn't know what he wanted to do. He didn't know how to apply himself. He left MNCS and went to [a local high school] and excelled—top of his class. He wasn't self-motivated. He needed help and direction" (Cecilia).

5. Offer more guidance on writing skills during their first few research projects and provide instruction on note- and test-taking skills right before graduation: In regard to curriculum, the college students identified three academic skill areas where they would have liked additional preparation: writing, note taking, and test taking. While all the graduates completed several research papers, wrote poetry, and composed essays at MNCS, they expressed feeling "a bit shaky" regarding their writing skills. "To this day, I still struggle with writing. I never studied it at school" (Bill). Graduates also felt they needed instruction in note and test taking to ensure their success at the postsecondary institutions they were attending where lecture are still the predominant teaching method. "Just research I'm good at. I am also good at setting up my deadlines, but I don't know how to study for tests" (Jamie). Marissa explains that she "wasn't prepared for note-taking and tests and large classes. I couldn't keep up."

However, while the graduates did offer these concrete suggestions, they were worried that the need for improvement in these areas might be used as a rationale for making fundamental changes to MNCS' structure. They clearly felt it was more important for students to choose and develop their own projects. "For all its issues and problems, I wouldn't change it, it influenced me positively" (Bill).

RECOMMENDATIONS FOR FUTURE RESEARCH

This study presented us with more questions than answers. First, how would learners in a traditional school environment compare to MNCS students on the presurvey assessment? We suspect that students who chose MNCS would rate themselves higher on the five skill areas (project-based skills, individual responsibility, resilience/persistence, reflection, and relationship skills) addressed in this survey than would a comparable sample of learners from a traditional school environment. This could have significance for MNCS if it is found that indeed MNCS does attract a unique portion of the overall student population. Conducting a comparative study of MNCS students and students in a traditional educational environment is also warranted. Several other subquestions resulted.

Another question arose as we were contacting students for interviews and we inadvertently talked with their parents. Parents' insights provided a different lens and would be a rich element in a future study. Also, we were intrigued by the students' reporting that their peers in the traditional school and some adults made disparaging and even hostile remarks about MNCS. Since school reform is more likely to thrive with community support, it would be interesting to explore this further. Finally, the graduates' perception that advisers perceived their roles quite differently led us to wonder how a nontraditional school might successfully orient and support teachers who experienced only more traditional school models.

CONCLUDING COMMENTS AND DISCUSSION

This study of the graduates of MNCS, a 7–12 charter school that has no formal classes but rather supports student-directed projects, sought to understand the school's effects on their project-based skills, individual responsibility, resilience/persistence skills, reflection skills, and relationship skills. Through survey and interviews, we found the MNCS graduates were articulate in identifying their strengths in each of these areas, some of which they felt they already possessed before attending MNCS and others they agreed they learned or had developed further. Graduates and researchers identified additional areas of growth due to the unique structure of this school. Recommendations for improving the school also emerged from this study.

The graduate's reaction to MNCS ranged from wildly supportive to disappointment, yet all expressed positive feelings having attended this unique school. The MNCS graduates concur that the project-based approach, allowing for choice of projects and constructing their own knowledge, is a more effective model for learning than the model found in traditional schools:

> All the annoying stuff is gone—bells, seats, mind on and mind off every forty-five minutes. And even then, your mind is mindless most of the time. Nine teachers a day, lockers, all of it gone . . . [and in its place is] a different environment so that learning is relevant and interesting (Marisa).

REFERENCES

Ancess, J. (1998). Urban dreamcatchers: Planning and launching new small schools. In M. Fine & J. I. Somerville (Eds.), *Small schools, big imaginations: A creative look at urban public schools* (pp. 22–35). Chicago: Cross City Campaign for Urban School Reform.

Drew, D. P. (2001, May 21). Minnesota New Country School finds niche in uncharted waters. Minneapolis Star Tribune,

Gladden, R. (1998). The small school movement: A review of the literature. In M. Fine and J. I. Somerville (Eds.), *Small schools, big imaginations: A creative look at urban public schools* (pp. 113–137). Chicago: Cross City Campaign for Urban School Reform.

Graba, J. (2001, April 25). *Why public education's future depends on new schools.* A speech delivered at Citizen's League Mind-Opener Meeting, St. Paul, Minnesota.

Gray, P., & Chanoff, D. (1986, February). Democratic schooling: What happens to young people who have charge of their own education? *American Journal of Education, 94,* 182–213.

Raywid, M. A. (1999, January). *Current literature on small schools.* ERIC Digest. EDO-RC-98-8. Retrieved at http:://www.ael.org/eric/digests/edorc988.html.

Thomas, D. (2003). *Little did we know: Ten years in the making of the Minnesota New Country School.* Retrieved from http://www.edvisions.coop/html/thomas_chapter.html.

Thomas, D., Anderson, J., Bartusek, M., Borwege, K., Kroehler, K., Lind, D., Pilling, M. A., Schmidt, J., Sonnek, A., & Swenson, K. (2001, September 15). A study of the Minnesota New Country School, District #4007: The seventh year. Published by MNCS.

10

Constituting a Democratic Learning Community: The Avalon Experience

Carrie Bakken and Andrea Martin, with Caitlin Rude

> We, the People of Avalon, in order to provide for a safe and productive learning environment, promote the obtaining and using of knowledge for the benefit of those around us, and ensure general happiness, do ordain and establish this constitution for Avalon high school.
>
> —Preamble to the Avalon High School Constitution

> Really we were already completely democratic before our constitution; student self-interest is central to the school—student choice is a student right and responsibility to do as well as you can, a kind of freedom when it is based upon your personal choice.
>
> —Caitlin Rude, senior, Avalon High School

Avalon High School in St. Paul was organized in 2001 by a group of parents who wanted to create a small "people-centered" postsecondary preparatory school of "outstanding character." In their search for teachers (and they attracted hundreds of inquiries), they advertised by asking, "What if teachers could design the ideal school? We can!" They were "seeking passionate, inspired, and hardworking individuals to build an imaginative, creative, and disciplined learning community." The school would be characterized by teacher ownership, collaborative teaching and decision making, highly innovative curricula, a small learning community, teacher development as a priority, and a truly supportive community.

Following the Minnesota New Country School model, Avalon became a teacher-owned school and a member of the EdVisions cooperative. Avalon became a learning community combining a college prep focus, interdisciplinary seminars, and a strong technology component all centered on project learning and the Minnesota graduation standards. This approach is complemented by extensive development individually and as a community in ethics and conflict resolution, interpersonal and life skills, and active citizenship and community service.

In its founding documents, Avalon states that it will "build a school culture and a set of values centered on excellence and active citizenship" and that it will "develop leadership opportunities for all participants. All members of the school community will be involved in decision-making, and students will be given a real voice and stake in the school." The founders, who also created the Twin Cities Academy Middle School several years earlier, were guided by the Basic School model of Ernest Boyer and the Carnegie Foundation for the Advancement of Teaching.

Though the model was designed for early primary, the founders believed that if students had attended a Basic School through their elementary years, Avalon should be the perfect high school learning community for them because of the emphasis on strong interpersonal relationships and the virtues of democratic character, a project focus on active learning and interdisciplinary study, and a participatory learning community where students were, at the center, joined by parents as partners and teachers as leaders.

Boyer speaks to essential conditions for creating authentic, democratic learning communities. He identifies six qualities of human interaction that are vital for creating authentic learning communities where every member is known: by name, by interests, by dispositions, by unique personhood, by contributions, and by productions. An authentic learning community would be a place with these qualities: purposeful, caring, disciplined, celebrative, communicative, and just:

> The basic school is, above all else, a community for learning, a place where staff and students, along with parents, have a shared vision of what the institution is seeking to accomplish. There is simply no way to achieve educational excellence in a school where purposes are blurred, where teachers and students fail to communicate thoughtfully with others, and

where parents are uninvolved in the education of their children. Community is, without question, the glue that holds an effective school together. (Boyer 1995, 18)

The founders of Avalon were also influenced by the philosophy of Jean Piaget, the great theorist of human development who advocated both an activity pedagogy and collaborative learning environments where students worked together to meet both personal and collective needs. He once remarked that each classroom should have two rooms—one for the teacher and student and one for just the students who earned the right to be free from adult constraints and autonomous among peers. Piaget based many of his later ideas for school communities on the 1948 Universal Declaration of Human Rights; likewise, the founding parents wanted Avalon to be as inclusive as possible contributing to an integrative (rather than desegregated) society. Article 26 of the declaration reads in part,

> Education shall be directed toward the full development of the human personality and to the strengthening of respect for human rights and fundamental freedoms. It shall promote understanding, tolerance and friendship among all nations, racial or religious groups, and shall further the activities of the United Nations for the maintenance of peace.

In interviews with the original school founders, it is very clear that they began with a specific definition of citizenship based on the work of Harry Boyte and the Center of Democracy and Citizenship, a learning place in grassroots civic leadership. From *Reinventing Citizenship: The Practice of Public Work*, governance and citizenship is defined as government not simply for us but of us and by us. Nor is citizenship simply voting and volunteering, for active citizenship is foremost leadership and public problem solving by ordinary folk:

> Active, public citizenship begins and is grounded in our everyday institutional environments—the places we live and work, go to school, volunteer, participate in communities of faith. It is public-spirited and practical: not utopian or immaculate but part of the messy, difficult, give-and-take process of problem solving. Citizenship links our daily life and interests to larger public values and arenas. Through citizenship we build and exercise our power. (Boyte 1995, 8)

More specifically, politics is understood as citizen politics, grounded in our daily institutional environments in public work, that is, collaborative civic work that is visible and significant to its stakeholders:

> Active citizenship is tied to an understanding of public life as diverse, contentious, and linked to, but distinct from, private and communal life. Thus the role of the citizen can connect people across lines of difference for the purpose of governing and problem solving, drawing on distinct cultural identities and other communities. (Boyte 1995, 8)

Avalon's stated mission, that "Avalon School is a strong, nurturing community that inspires active learning, local action, and global awareness," captures the essence of the school: a school where teachers and students take ownership of their work. In the following pages, we conclude with the voices of students and teachers regarding their congress and school constitution.

STUDENT PERSPECTIVES FROM INTERVIEWS AND REFLECTION PAPERS

The Avalon Constitution and Congress were originally created in a block seminar called "Creating the Avalon Constitution." About twenty of us students and Carrie (Bakken, an adviser and seminar leader) thought we could do it in one block (term), but it took two blocks to complete it. It was so difficult. It was painfully put together, constituted if you will. Why? Because of all the arguments and deliberations over wording and meaning and trying to be consistent. I recently read that when the founding fathers (and mother, let's not forget Abigail Adams) knew more what each didn't want than what they wanted together, they weren't sure at the constitutional meetings what they would come up with. You can see this quite clearly in the Federalist Papers. Some wanted to limit the rights of citizens, some wanted ordinary citizens to govern, and others wanted consent of the governed through representation. This was very difficult work and it took years. We took months.

Well, we were like that constitutional convention. At one point we locked ourselves in a room for two days every week and deliberated. There were so many perspectives and needs and wants. It was amazing really.

There was lots of debate about who governs, who makes decisions, who's got the power. We took the U.S. Constitution as our model.

Do we see connections between what we did and our constitution and what the original founders did and created? Well those men had little to follow—the Articles of Confederation and knowledge of the Iroquois nation's government, I believe. Our school constitution is based on the U.S. Constitution—it is the one we live under and the constitution most familiar to us. We looked at other schools, but most weren't constituted with an actual constitution document, plus we have different structures and different needs. We did have the Paideia School's constitution, Walter's old school, and it was helpful to see that students could actually write a constitution. And they were younger (middle school); it is amazing to find out that constitution at Paideia is about thirty years old and has stood the test of time and has been amended, too. But we really needed our own, for we too are unique.

The Avalon Congress is open to all; usually at the weekly convening of the Congress, there is one adviser and ten to fifteen kids (about 15 percent) on a regular basis. Probably 50 to 60 percent are interested in the Congress's deliberations in some concrete way. One example of increased involvement was when maybe 30 to 40 percent of the school showed up when we were debating the pledge of allegiance in school.

Why is the Congress important? It allows student input on specific issues and general ones, too; also, everyone, including staff, can have a voice. The Congress and the constitution are really needed on a large scale (such as large schools), but on a small scale it depends on how people really get along; you don't need rules until you need them. On a small scale here at Avalon, we resolve issues one on one or with peer meditation; most issues between people are how to resolve issues and create a respectful environment.

Really we were already completely democratic before our constitution; students' self-interest is central to the school—student choice is a student right, and responsibility to do as well as you can is a kind of freedom when it is based on your personal choice. School life is not simply framed in terms of right and wrong with only one group having all the authority and power; teachers are leaders here—there isn't the hierarchy existing in traditional schools. Any member of this community can bring an issue to the school board or to teachers or to the student body. This is a trusting place where you are who you are and you can be who you want to be.

One of our strengths is peer mediation and restorative circles. Usually we somehow go through this and agree to disagree or agree to agree; most "cases" are usually where someone says something mean or stupid, not violence, and mediation "clears the air."

Our culture is being a small place organized around interpersonal relationships: good community, one on one, small groups, good relationships. But you have to work at making it a good place. It doesn't just happen. Just because you're small doesn't make you a great school. If you have a school of 500 or 1,500, you need formal structures, rules, and procedures, especially around authority, power, and status. A constitution in a school of 150 is going to be different than in a school of 2,000 because in a school of 150 everyone knows each other and you are "constituted" not by laws but by relationships between people who know, tolerate, and respect each other.

The great thing with our constitution is you can amend it; you can change the actual constitution, as school is ever changing and is a peaceful place. So we changed the judiciary—the judges had no cases. Anyway, with a judicial system you had litigation and a verdict—a poor way, really, to resolve issues.

TEACHER VOICES FROM CONVERSATIONS AND INTERVIEWS

Almost every person in the Constitution Seminar, in their reflection paper, responded to the fundamental question, How much power can students really have? The most contentious issue in the whole process of writing the constitution was "should the school staff (adults) have executive veto power over the Congress or legislative branch (which is open to all school members, students and staff alike)." We talked a lot about in loco parentis, that we staff were professional educators, legally responsible for students' safety and well-being. Legally, and particularly in such a litigious culture, parents trusted the staff to care for and protect students. Some students countered with "If you really trust us we should be able to make all decisions." Others understood their role as students. Though interest was shown in the school's budget and personnel practices, they were less interested in being accountable for all decisions. They needed to know they were being heard. They needed to know they had choices and could make many decisions. And that was power!

The creation of the constitution was a message to students that teachers honored their input and leadership. We teachers saw ourselves as authoritative, not authoritarian, and students were in school to learn many things. But running a school was not at the top of the list. In setting up our school, constituting it if you will, we saw the creation of the school constitution as a powerful way to build the culture of community.

Both students and teachers take ownership and responsibility. It becomes a way to re-create the traditional roles of teacher and student. This is not a place where students have to react to traditional roles. As the Congress and school matured, it became obvious that if a student or teacher wanted to change something, it is up to the Congress to make it happen. What a powerful lesson in citizenship, in civics, in civility. As a civics teacher trained as a lawyer, I observed that community building and understanding were a result of this project. The students learned to negotiate, debate, listen, reformulate, compromise, vote, and then move on to the next aspect of formulating the document. The process also included learning much about articulating ideas; students learned the whole purpose of words and logical reasoning and how words and arguments can be misconstrued or misinterpreted from the original intent.

We find it interesting and not surprising that the whole constitution project mirrors the surrounding society. Both students and teachers expect more of the Congress—resolving issues and solving more problems. Congress sometimes proclaims an action but does not follow through; it promises to tackle an issue but fails to do so in a timely fashion or with appropriate resolve. Similar to our own government, there is lots of talk; laws are passed that are either unfunded mandates or empty promises. There is some apathy or indifference, and only a small portion of students are actually involved in congressional issues. But if the issue has a relevant significance, such as the question of a dress code or the question of whether we say the pledge of allegiance or whether we have a prom, a greater number participate. On the other hand, so many Congress participants are involved in active citizenship through service learning. For example, many students volunteered for the Wellstone campaign, whose headquarters was a mile from the school.

In congressional meetings, we often joke that we Americans complain and believe that being vocal is enough, in fact consider it a form of active citizenship. But if you want to change something at Avalon, you go through the Congress. We did in fact amend the original constitution. Originally we had a judiciary. We also established peer mediation and the restorative justice circle. Some faculty had experience in restorative justice and alternative dispute resolution. So litigation was not the choice. We did not believe in winner versus loser.

The original judges were, except for one female student, white males who were bored and without purpose. They complained and kept conjuring up plans to "take over." For example, the judges considered investigating the "probable" misuse of computers by other students, as the advisers had too many other things to do. It was difficult for them initially to understand that they could not usurp the teachers' legal responsibilities and that possible suspensions involved privacy rights.

This is a holistic community; it is a nonpunitive, win–win democracy at work in all its glory and imperfections. Students learn to be active citizens by living it out. Choosing not to participate and vote in fact becomes a right; but it is our hope that having a working constitution and a Congress will actually increase student and teacher understanding that active citizenship is a responsibility to self and to the commonwealth.

APPENDIX: THE CONSTITUTION OF THE SCHOOL OF AVALON

Preamble

We, the People of Avalon, in order to provide for a safe and productive learning environment, promote the obtaining and usage of knowledge for the benefit of those around us, and ensure general happiness, do ordain and establish this constitution for Avalon high school.

Article I: The Legislative Branch

Section I

All Legislative power herein shall be vested in a Congress of Avalon, which shall consist solely of that group of officials.

Section II: Congress: Organization and Powers of Impeachment

1. Congress is made up of any person choosing to take part.
2. Any person attending may vote, regardless of prior attendance. The only reason a person would not be allowed to vote is if that person were removed from Congress.
3. For a person to be removed there must be a majority vote in favor of removing that person. Length of removal will be judged by remaining Congress members. If a person is removed three times, the person is no longer allowed to take part in Congress.
4. No representative shall hold a position of higher power within the Congress, therefore, there shall be no Speaker of the House, nor any similar position.

Section III: Meetings of Congress

Meetings shall be held on a weekly basis, at whatever time is found convenient by the members of Congress (if there is free attendance we need a set time).

Section IV: Rules of Procedure

Minutes must be recorded at every meeting. The Person that records minutes at one meeting leads at the next.

Section V: Privileges and Limitations

1. Representatives of Congress shall be compensated with credit, and by no other means.
2. For a Congress member who has been removed three times to be reinstated, that member must first go through mediation, as well as be approved by Congress.

Section VI: Procedures for Passing Bills, Executive Veto

1. Congress is charged with passing bills.
2. Any member of the school may propose a bill to the Legislative body, whether they are a student or a staff member.

3. A bill must pass through Congress with a majority, after which it must be passed through the Executive branch, also with a majority vote.
4. For a bill to be vetoed there must be a majority vote within the Executive branch in favor of such a veto.
5. A bill may not be re-proposed for one block.

Section VII: Powers Delegated to Congress

1. The Representatives of the student body shall report all meeting information to their peers.
2. Congress may make, modify, or disband any law applying to students or the student/advisor relationship so long as it is unconstitutional or against any higher-level laws.
3. Congress reserves the right to declare emergency or follow up meetings that are not scheduled.
4. Congress may form committees to organize, control, and lead any and all social events, including but not limited to the All School Meetings, Presentation nights, Public Relations tours, School Dances, and other events called to order.

Section VIII: Powers Denied to Congress

1. Congress may not override decisions made by higher-level laws, including, but not limited to the School Board, School District, Minnesota Government, or US Federal Law.
2. Congress may not be involved in or perform any disciplinary actions, as those are reserved for the Mediators.
3. Congress may not override the Executive veto
4. Congress may not place restrictions on other branches of Government.

Article II: The Judiciary Branch

Section 1: Division of Branch, Tenure of Office

1. The Judiciary branch of Avalon should consist of the Mediation Council.
2. The Mediation Council will consist of Peer Mediators as well as the Circle Process Group.

3. Any student who attends the mediation training may be a Mediator.
4. Mediators will facilitate communication to resolve individual student/ student or student/advisor issues.
5. There will be a minimum of three trained Peer Mediators.
6. The Circle Process Group will address school issues through a Talking Circle and bring resolutions to Congress.

Section II: Jurisdiction

1. The Judicial Branch will be committed to Restorative Justice
2. The Judicial Branch will handle all cases that are not in violation of higher laws.

Article III: Executive Branch

1. The Avalon staff shall form the Executive Branch
2. The Executive Branch shall be responsible for upholding all higher laws.
3. The Executive Branch is permitted to veto laws made by Congress.
4. It is the responsibility of the Executive Branch to enforce the laws.

Article IV: Governing Body

Avalon School guarantees all students a democratic single-party government, and will follow all procedures as such.

Article V: Amendment Procedures

Any member of the school may propose an amendment, or bill, whether they are students or staff, to the Legislative Branch.

First Amendment: Bill of Rights and Responsibilities

1. Every person has the right to bring someone to mediation.
2. Every person has the responsibility to attend mediation when asked at a reasonable time.
3. Every person has the right to be treated with respect and dignity.

4. Every person has the responsibility to treat others with respect and dignity.
5. Every person has the right to her or his own personal space.
6. Every person has the responsibility to respect other people's personal space.
7. Every person has the right and responsibility to try.
8. Every person has the right to ask why.
9. Every person has the responsibility to question themselves and their actions in times of duress.
10. Every person has the right to speak and communicate her or his views as long as they are respectful to others.
11. Every person has the responsibility to listen at all times to whoever is speaking.
12. Every person has the right and responsibility to be involved and participate here at Avalon High School.

REFERENCES

Boyer, E. (1995). *The basic school*. Princeton, NJ: Carnegie Foundation for the Advancement of Teaching.

Boyte, H. (1995). *Reinventing citizenship—The practice of public work*. St. Paul: University of Minnesota Extension.

11

Why Are These Schools Cool?
Voices of the Students and Parents

Ron Newell*

The secret of education lies in respecting the pupil. It is not for you to choose what he shall know, what he shall do. It is chosen and foreordained, and only he holds the key to his own secret.

—Ralph Waldo Emerson

Lynn Stoddard, in his book *Educating for Human Greatness*, explains that there are three inherent core drives within each human:

The drive to be a recognized "somebody" (Identity). This drive is much more than the need to merely survive or exist. It is an intense need of the human spirit to fulfill one's unique potential as a special contributor to the world. It is a need to count for something, to have a sense of self-worth. It is a drive to answer the questions, who am I? Why do I exist? And what is the purpose of my life? It is a never-ending quest for Identity.

The drive for warm human relationships (Interaction). This drive confirms another well-known characteristic of human nature—we are all born with a need to love and be loved. Everyone feels a deep need to *belong* and have a sense of community with other human beings. We have a built-in need to communicate with others. This is the second most powerful motivating force of human nature. It is the force of Interaction.

*With contributions from advisers, students, and parents of Agriculture and Food Sciences Academy (Little Canada, MN), Avalon Charter School (St. Paul, MN), Explore Knowledge Academy (Henderson, NV), High School for the Recording Arts (St. Paul, MN), Harbor City International School (Duluth, MN), Minnesota New Country School (Henderson, MN), New Century Charter School (Hutchinson, MN), RiverBend Academy (Mankato, MN), and Valley New School (Appleton, WI).

The drive for truth and knowledge (Inquiry). Human beings are born cu-
rious. They are born with a strong drive to make sense of the world and to
acquire personal knowledge and wisdom. Curiosity is the third most powerful motivating force of human nature. It is the force of personal Inquiry.
(Stoddard 2003, 27–28)

Stoddard (2003) goes on to say, "If these innate drives are universal, as it
appears they are, it means we can hold children responsible for their own
learning and development. Everyone is designed for greatness" (28).

As a result of the recognition of these truths, Stoddard came to the conclusion that the school curriculum has become the end, not the means, of
schooling and learning. Parents and children seek identity, interaction, and
inquiry, not canned lessons, time-based courses, and Carnegie units. We at
EdVisions know this to be true. When we visit the schools founded on the
personalized project-based approach, we continually hear similar responses. This chapter is a compilation of the voices of students and parents expressing the effects of these "cool schools." Listen to these voices
and see that Stoddard's observations ring true.

Among the comments from students and parents, you will see a number of attributes expressed: a sense of community, the freedom and responsibility fostered by the learning program, and the feeling students
have for each other and for their adviser and teachers. All of those bespeak
of valuing identity, interaction, and inquiry. The comments are divided by
the three categories Stoddard mentions as being most important in a student's education. We will begin with a sense of identity.

IDENTITY

When students were asked what element of their schools determined it to
be a "cool school," most identified freedom. But freedom comes in many
guises, one of them being allowed to be your own individual. "I can go to
school being bold about my beliefs and who I am," said one student. Another indicated his school "lets you be you," another "this is a great school
because the students get to be themselves." Several commented that it was
not only their individual freedom, but "all the students at this school are
so free in personality. Also they don't really care what anyone thinks
about them." This means that peer pressures that cause many problems in

large schools are no longer menacing. When individuals are allowed free expression, there is less negative talk.

As others put it, "You can be yourself and not care what others have to say." Another's expression: "Everyone has their own personality and their unique ideas. This school has its own perspective for each individual. I am only a freshman here and I already have set goals for my future." Another student described their school as cool because "there are a lot of very interesting people at this school" and "there is a mix of different personalities at this school."

Parents echoed these comments about identity: "What a wonderful opportunity you have given us—a school where the kids don't fit a stereotype and the teachers care about everyone," said one parent. Another said, "The change has been great for my son. I feel that my son is appreciated for who he is." One student sums it up by stating, "At other schools we were treated like we were little kids and here we are treated more like adults and that makes me feel safer and it makes me feel like I can do more."

Another aspect of identity is demonstrated by teachers who "treat each student individually—it is great quality for a school to have. Students need that kind of attention." Teachers deal with students in a totally different capacity—one of adviser and facilitators rather than as directive authoritarians. Consequently, as another student remarked, "We get to have personal relationships with our teachers." Additional comments validating the importance of identity are "You get more one-on-one learning," and "You also have more of a friendly relationship with your advisor and teachers. The teachers understand problems that students have and instead of telling them to deal with it, they take the time to talk to the student about the problem and help with ways to solve it or make the situation better."

Also, the schools exhibit valuing student identity by allowing students choice in the learning program. Because the schools are primarily about self-directed learning, each student chooses the content of their projects from their interests. Rather than curriculum driven, the projects are authentic and realistic to the students. From this process, students "learn more responsibility because they aren't being told what to do, they're set free." Additional comments were made regarding freedom to choose the manner of learning:

"As a student you have a say in what goes on."

"I can learn about whatever I want to learn about and I can get credit for projects in the summer and at home."

"I get to plan my day rather than have someone else plan it for me."

"I can study what I want. There are no required classes where I have to listen to a teacher lecture. There is a lot more independence, which I appreciate very much."

"It gives us a chance to learn the things that we actually want to learn."

"I get to learn more stuff I need for future careers."

"We have the opportunity to do things differently."

Not only do students have the choice of subject matter and study time, but they learn to be responsible as a result of the project process. "It is up to you to get your own education or not," exclaims one student. "You get to make or break your education—it is in your hands," said another. Because "it is more on you to get your work done," students feel valued for their contributions.

Another aspect of identity is the fact that students may work at an individual pace and not be captive to the time-based curriculum. "It has helped me be more responsible and allows me to work on my own schedule," said one student. "You can take your time and not feel rushed," said another. "I am more successful at this school than my other school because I am working at my own pace and I don't have to stop at a certain time and switch subjects." "We don't have homework unless we want to," said one student. "We can choose our own projects, and you don't have to go from class to class and learn about boring subjects." One student said, "We have more individual rights and we can work at our own pace," thereby linking rights to decisions about timeliness of learning. Having the rights to work at an individual pace is so powerful that one student said, "I wake up and want to go to school because you can work at your own pace." Another said, "The fact that I am in control of my future and of what I want to learn keeps me motivated to continue working." Following are additional powerful statements:

"This school is different from other schools because we don't just sit around in a classroom and listen to what teachers are saying and then be expected to memorize it all and take a test. Here we're given a chance to learn what we want and make a product we want. I don't know about other students here, but that really makes a difference!"

"Advisers will guide you on what you need to do when a teacher will tell you what you have to do. The choices we make become the outcome for daily life. I like the independence. I think that if a student can work independently that they can achieve anything, they can accomplish anything they want. When I was in the normal school I didn't know what I wanted to do. Now I am interested in computer technology, networking, and other things. I really like the opportunities at this school."

"I think the thing I would miss the most, were I to switch schools, would be not needing permission to do things such as use the bathroom or get a drink of water. If, at a high school level, we are expected to make decisions that will affect our whole lives, say choosing a college, why can't we pee without permission?"

"I love being able to work on projects that interest me and keep me wanting to learn more about everything. I feel sorry for people who are not able to do what they want and learn about things they find fascinating."

Being acknowledged for having a separate identity certainly can be a strong motivator. A strong sense of identity leads to self-efficacy and success. "I am more successful at this school because I will be studying what I need to learn for what I want to become."

When a student said, "I can be who I am," they speak for all students of EdVisions schools. Their identities matter. They do not have to become automatons and one of the anonymous dots in the middle of the bell curve.

INTERACTION

The theme of freedom is expressed in many of the comments. This is certainly true for the concept of interaction. EdVisions schools are inherently choice ridden and democratic as a result of being organized around small-group advisories, individual and small-group projects, group assessments, and place-based learning. In addition, they are organized around student-directed projects, not classes. Students determine their schedules according to their learning activities, not around what teachers design.

Advisories are usually in a ratio of 1 to 18, and school sizes are generally 100 to 150 students. This small size allows for more interaction between advisers and students, students and students, and advisers and parents. Not only is identity valued, but so is the interaction of student to student, student to adviser, and student to community. Students therefore express themselves more freely, make decisions more often, and experience more verbal interaction than in traditional schools. Some of the comments pertaining to the freedom allowed students include the following:

"I think that learning in an environment that allows freedom can give a person choices that they would not have in a 'normal' school."

"This school is a good helpful way to learn and study different subjects the way you want to learn them, and I think that is the best way to learn."

"Because I can choose what I want to do; the school does not choose what I have to do."

"To have freedom is what everyone (kid and adult) is looking for, and I think to have that makes school so much better and I actually look forward to going to school."

"You have more freedom to do what you are really interested in through your projects."

"[This school] opens opportunities you would never think of. It gives you more of an independent learning basis which helps you lead your life as an independent person. It also shows a lot more career opportunities and broadens your horizons. The best thing is the free will, because you have a choice in what you do and not just your subject to do what 'the teacher knows is best.'"

This concept of free will is not only about identity but also about interactions allowed by the school setting. When a school establishes a routine for the purpose of setting students free to choose, a new dynamic creates new relationships between teachers and students. Students choose the content and the time of their learning, and teachers become advisers rather than deliverers of content. This freedom allows students to create both their own learning time and space:

"By far my favorite aspect of this school is the independence students get. In attending a project-based school, I have the freedom to study what I want when I want to. For instance, this morning, at the end of math class, I was just learning something new and I didn't want to stop so I didn't. I continued working on math for the next hour, too. Not only do I have the freedom to manage my own time here, but I also have the freedom to study what I want."

But simply having the time to learn what they want can be daunting. Some students recognized that they had to accept the responsibility to use their time wisely:

"[This school] has a lot more freedom but you have to be really responsible and don't abuse it or you'll get behind and it's hard to catch up."

"For one thing, I enjoy the freedom that I have here. I can learn about the things that I want to learn about. Of course, with freedom comes responsibility and at times, it is difficult to get everything done and stay on task all of the time."

"On the other hand, the worst thing about going to [this school] would also have to be the freedom that I have. The downside to freedom is the responsibility. It was not terribly difficult for me to come to [this school] because I am a responsible person. However, I have seen many people who took advantage of the freedom they received and never did anything school related. Being responsible for your own education is something most people don't even think about until they're in college. Having that responsibility at a younger age than most is sometimes difficult for me because it adds a little bit of extra stress around school. Overall though, I enjoy being responsible and having freedom in my education. I feel prepared to go to college and learn what I want to know so I can become the person I want to be."

Students concluding wise use of time attests to the fact that they have learned to become self-directed learners. That is why these schools are constructed the way they are and why the interactions are built on individual student needs, not on teacher needs. In allowing freedom for students to choose content, a distinct interaction occurs.

The primary interaction, however, is the way the schools value the adolescent need for acceptance and community. The feeling of acceptance was a frequent response made by students. "It is a small school and I just love small schools because then you know just about everyone," remarked one student. Another student said, "I also like how most of the students get along and everybody knows everybody." A large part of this acceptance is evidence of caring and the lack of bullying: "There are not any cliques at [this school]," said one student; "I enjoy this school because I don't have to put up with bullies," exclaimed another. "You could get picked on during normal school but not much here," remarked another student. Another student was more inclusive: "This school is nice. At my other schools there was a lot of fighting, cussing and the teachers were mean. Here there is no fighting and the teachers are better."

The small communities and caring atmospheres lead to development of friendships: "I have awesome friends in this small school. I know so many people, and I get along with a lot of them," said one student. "Everyone is very nice and I'm just about friends with everyone," said another." Some reacted to the nongraded programs: "I also like how most of the students get along and everybody knows everybody. It gives the younger students a chance to interact with older students and vice versa." Another student had this to say: "There are no grades, and we all work together. I mean a six-teen-year-old and a thirteen-year-old can do a project together without feel-ing weird." These friendships extend beyond just being pals. It also refers to friendships made between students and advisers: one student refers to an adviser as "my friend—for the last couple of weeks we have been best of friends."

Many students referred to the small atmosphere created by the learning communities in more general terms: "I think this is the greatest school be-cause of the atmosphere and the people in it. All the kids and advisers are so nice and easy to talk to. Everyone is so friendly and thoughtful." And yet another remarked, "You will pretty much know everyone you go to school with and will have better interaction with the teacher." One student said, "[This school] is the coolest school in America because everyone there is nice and we all get along."

Others noted the small size of groups or classes had benefits: "This is a good school if you have a hard time learning in big groups. The teachers have smaller classes than most public schools, so they can work with you more one on one." With smaller groupings, "the staff can pay more atten-tion to each kid." Another remarked, "I also like how when you ask a question here the teacher has time to explain it because there is a better student-to-teacher ratio."

With the smaller ratios of students to teacher, "if you need help the teacher will give you help, and you will learn it instead of never under-standing your work." Another student said, "If you are having a hard time understanding something, you get the one-on-one help you need." By having this one-on-one help, "advisers help you do better." Two students referred to the difference between the small EdVisions learning commu-nity and a previous school: "I can get more help than last year," said one.

"This school is a lot different from the last one I attended because it is smaller so the teachers actually get a chance to help the students with their work when they need it," exclaimed another. One student referred to help coming from not only the advisers: "Whether it is between students or a student and a teacher, there will always be several people willing to help you."

The small communities lead to a feeling of safety: "With the small amount of people, I feel like I can concentrate more," said one student. Another said that "the environment is different here. It just feels a lot safer." And there were comments from students noting the family-like atmosphere of their schools: "Our school doesn't seem like much if you just look at the building, but if you come inside and join our school it's like we are one big happy family." Another student recognized that the small atmosphere leads to more inclusion of family: "I also think that [this school] is cool because the teachers get to know your family where in a larger school the only thing you know about that teacher is his or her last name." The small, caring, family-like atmosphere leads to better results for students.

Many students referred to their teacher and advisers as being caring and concerned about them: "I like this school because the teachers are nice," said one. "There are friends and teachers who care about you and also the kids here look out for one another, and are good people," remarked another. "The other schools I attended were huge and the teachers didn't have time for you," said another. Probably the most telling comment was, "Instead of a nagging teacher, you have advisors who help when help is needed. That takes some of the pressure off and you can learn and accomplish more." Another powerful statement:

"We don't have teachers constantly making us feel like we're in a hurry to get stuff done when we can choose how much time *we* want to spend on it. I think it is a good thing that these teachers finally got sick of pushing kids around and decided that there's a different way to learn. Old schoolteachers are just teaching kids not to be independent. They constantly tell the kids what to do, where to go and when to get there. They don't let the kids speak for themselves. They shouldn't like teaching like that."

It appears the students clearly understand the difference between an adviser and a traditional schoolteacher. Two other comments bear that out: "There are teachers here who really believe in what they are doing. They are willing to help us as students to succeed. They will take their time to make sure you understand something" and "The teachers really seem to care about you, they are more like friends than big mean grumpy teachers. I do believe that having an advisor makes your feelings be more understood." Because of the small school size, the advisory system, and small groupings, each individual student receives the help he or she needs to succeed.

The primary point of interaction is to develop a sense of trust and respect for our fellow man. Some of the student comments were quite mature in recognizing the effect of positive interactions: "The students are respectful and the teachers help us to the best of their abilities," said one student. Another student recognized that "it is a relaxed environment and even if you make a fool of yourself, everyone still loves you." Another said, "In this school people accept me for who I am." Another comment was, "Everyone is so polite."

These students are recognizing that the interactions incurred in the EdVisions learning communities are respectful, positive, affirming, and caring. This respect for the individual (identity) and the allowance of interaction contribute to the creation of students who become respectful and caring citizens. As a student said, "Later in life, the students who attended [this school] will know how important it is to treat others with respect, and treat each point of view equally. The world these days needs more people like that."

The previous comments exhibit a strong declaration for these types of small-school environments. There are too few school settings in which the students perceive their adviser and teacher as their friend and advocate, that induce the feeling of family, or that help develop trust and respect for each other. For the students to react with such strong sentiments of acceptance, friendship, trust, respect, and camaraderie is indeed heartwarming.

INQUIRY

The primary point made by student comments, again, had to do with freedom, in this case freedom to pursue an interest. Inquiry is a powerful tool for learning when a student is self-directed and therefore intrinsically motivated. From the large number of statements received regarding freedom of choice, some of the most powerful statements had to do with discovery: "I can explore areas I am interested in," said one student. "You can study or do a project on just about anything you're interested in" and "I like the fact we get to choose what we would like to learn about" are two other relevant comments. Students were more reflective about learning than they were about interaction and identity:

"[I like] the freedom we have to walk around and not feel confined to a classroom, the freedom to study what we want to learn and be able to use the information and expand on it and not have to go on to the next subject, and the freedom to go out into the community and learn from other people who already are experts in the field we are studying at the time."

"I have the freedom here to explore in all different directions — something most schools don't have. I can spend all day working on one project if I want to, or I can work on seven projects in a day."

"Projects can be fun and involve things that you actually enjoy. Instead of doing boring homework about things you don't care about and that you'll just forget after a test, you can do projects that are enjoyable and things that are interesting. The more something fits your individual interests the more likely you'll remember it and you will more likely work harder at completing it. At [this] school you will learn things that you will use for life instead of just forgetting them when you're out of school."

These statements exhibit the power of awe and wonder in learning. These students have recognized that following a teacher-driven curriculum does not result in the most effective learning. Allowing them to inquire into areas of interest led to learning more deeply and with greater motivation.

Others spoke of experiential learning:

"I agree that most learning is done through experience, and by doing activities and participating in educational things we are going to learn so much more."

"At the other school you do worksheets, and a lot of busy work. At our school you don't do busy work, you do things that you want to do and that you think are important."

"We learn in fun and exciting ways. We do hands-on learning and we do lots of fun field trips relating to core classes, or inspiring us to do projects."

"I am more successful because I think we have a lot more opportunities to get out of school and explore the world around us."

Projects are motivating for students. Because they determine their own project parameters, interest remains high and more is learned. Some related comments were the following:

"Our projects definitely deal with things we enjoy doing. My computer networking project deals with one of my possible career choices."

"The projects are good. I can choose anything that I want to learn about and do a project on it. It's a great way to learn. I can learn my own way."

"The best thing is I like choosing and teaching myself what I want to learn about. I like that *you* get to choose what *you* want to do for your project, when *you* want it to be due, and what *you* want it to look like! That is the best thing here. There are many more, but that is the best."

"I like doing projects of my choice, and the projects help me to learn better."

Choice is such a powerful human need. It is when we choose to learn that we actually engage in learning. In *Passion for Learning* (2003), I wrote that we learn something only when we perceive the need to learn it. These students have recognized the need to learn out of interest. From their interest they were able to deepen their study via inquiry while meeting state standards (and in many cases going beyond them).

Some students progressed beyond a mere interest; they became passionate about what they were doing:

"I had more fun doing this project than I had at Disney World when I was nine. I loved writing something that I was really passionate about, and reading about literature and parallels between stories and myths, and then thinking for a long time and trying to find a way for every bit of information that I received to fit into my thesis statement."

The previous comment was made by a fourteen-year-old. If only all ninth graders were that interested and passionate about inquiring into literature! Another comment:

"I did a project that let me do a hands-on study: my own research. In a normal class, I would have taken data from Professor Somebody-or-other's study and made conclusions based on that. Project-based learning let me do my study and create my own data. It made the project all the more relevant. I cared about what I was learning and what the final result was. The data was no longer strings of numbers crowding the page; now it was my time and energy showing something positive, an end result. It was my information, my labor, my project."

This ownership in the learning process is difficult to attain in the traditional setting. Students in the project-based schools of the EdVisions community speak with passion of their learning experiences.

They recognize the extent to which they are learning. Many commented on how much more they could learn in the student-driven project-based system:

"Project-based learning is a wonderful setup. Personally, I could do well in a 'normal' setup, but I enjoy PBL much more. I am able to learn about things that would not be mentioned in a typical school, and I am not restricted by what the state says I need to know. I learn important skills like time management and public speaking, which I think are much more important than knowing when Thomas Jefferson died. A really useful tool I have used is finding resources. At [this school] there are hardly any textbooks, so we have to find information on our own. I have learned much more about finding valid sources than I ever learned before and I know that this will help me in the long run."

Another student related how lack of interest became a more in-depth interest:

"The main reason I did not like history was because there are so many things to remember, and I did not know why I had to remember them other than what my teacher told me. Now that I know how deep history is, I can see myself finding some part in history interesting and wanting to learn more about it."

By inquiring into aspects of history of interest to the student, it became possible to learn to enjoy the depth and breadth of the subject. Two other comments exhibit another sort of in-depth learning:

"I have done projects varying from art creation to political activism. I think that project-based learning is great for high school students because it provides the structure and comfort that gives a solid base to build off of, but it also supplies resources and space to explore yourself and your place in the world. Attending a school where I have been given so much responsibility and freedom has helped me become a much more self-assured and reliable person."

"Project-based learning, I feel, is one of the most in-depth ways to learn about a topic. Not only do you have to be motivated on a personal level, in order to find the means necessary to begin, go through with, and complete a project, but you have to rely on your community, both within [the school] and outside of, in order to get from beginning to end. It's a wonderful way to encourage youth to be involved, to expand their minds, and to open up to all possibilities. As much as I hate grad standards, I must admit, I love seeing the creative ways people are able to achieve them. I love learning about what other people are doing and how motivated in my own projects I become. I enjoy the freedom and responsibility that project-based learning has to offer. The fact that I can structure a project that can take 500 hours or a project that takes 30 is wonderful, giving me opportunities I would not have had otherwise."

These two students are reacting to the ways project-based learning and the spirit of inquiry lead to an understanding of yourself and your world. Inquiry expands the mind and develops persistence. The freedom to formulate your own plan, find your own resources, and produce your own product results in powerful learning.

The students recognize the route to finished projects is not without obstacles. The passion, the awe, and the wonderment of learning are not consistently obvious. A well-rounded education comes with a price. The questioning and inquiring pedagogy, utilized at the EdVisions schools, also helps students realize the value of life skills such as determination and persistence:

"I think that project-based learning is a good thing for so many people and I really enjoy the project picking part. It just takes a lot of self-discipline, which is something that I know I have to work a little harder on."

Most students come to the conclusion at some time that project-based learning is not an easy way through high school. If they ignore the need for work and persistence, they may fail to graduate. But by coming to that realization, first by applying persistence through interests and the spirit of inquiry, they are then better equipped for the world. Another comment:

"This system is not, however, meant for everyone. It requires a lot of self-motivation. The majority of the work done during school hours is done completely separately from teachers. Students must be able to manage their time and stay on task. This has proven difficult for some students (including myself) and is, in my opinion, the flaw in the system. This possibility is rooted in independent learning, unfortunately, and could not be entirely removed without greatly compromising project-based learning. In my opinion the positive aspects of project-based learning outweigh the flaws, and it is a beneficial program for many."

This student's recognition of the need for discipline is typical of students' reflection after experiencing the EdVisions system for more than a year. The recognition of the need for self-discipline is the key to success in any endeavor. That is why it is necessary to initiate self-interests and a spirit of inquiry prior to "mandating" student learning. Regardless of students' initial thoughts, they eventually come to the same conclusion as the student quoted here:

"Coming from a traditional junior high and a brief period at a traditional high school I can honestly say that I greatly prefer the project-based learning style. Although most students may end up with a slightly-less-than-rounded four years, what they do study in that time will be learned in far greater detail due both to a student's interest and the flexibility within the topic itself. This is not to say, however, that a project-based student cannot get a rounded education; with some determination it is entirely possible to meet or even exceed the range of study provided by most schools. Our system can give a student access to areas of study rarely seen in traditional schools, especially in the arts and social sciences."

Or, as one student put it, "At my old school I wasn't learning anything. But here I am learning." That is the sum total of the power of inquiry — leading to the perception of increased understanding and learning of additional life skills that will contribute to their lifelong habits.

Many of the students stated they would not return to traditional ways of learning: "I *never* want to go back to the old way of being taught. I want to learn what I want to learn," said one. Others spoke of their passion for the school: "I used to count the days, hours, and seconds until that glorious day in June when I was finally free! As I sit here at [my school] I hardly care when school is over, and why is that? It is because of the freedom."

Yet others described the alternative as being daunting: "Without [this school] I would not be finishing school," said one student. "Without [this school] I would be overwhelmed with boredom," said another. And when a student says that "without [this school] I probably would have dropped out of school by now," you know that the experience of being valued as a human being, having freedom to choose what and when to learn, and developing trust and respect via the interactions of all members of the learning community was a powerful experience.

There were some statements made by parents that spoke to the power of valuing student identity, interaction, and inquiry. "It was like a light was turned on in our child since attending [the school]. She has grown, not just academically, but as an individual. She has become more confident, and in many ways more responsible. We think the positive relationships she has with both students and staff at [the school], and the fact that she is respected as an individual there, has done that for her."

Another parent stated that their "daughter likes school, enjoys learning through her projects, has truly grown emotionally (good friends, better self-esteem), and enjoys the classes offered by the school. We see a very helpful staff that is always friendly and willing to cope with any issue." Other comments by parents include the following:

"I have been amazed by the changes in my son's attitude and behavior throughout the year, to see how much he has progressed in such a small amount of time. I would have to say that it is due to the different teaching methods of the [school] staff, and the ideas of letting children make some decisions about their education."

"It is extremely encouraging to hear the change in our son's attitude toward learning and school! He speaks very highly of his teachers . . . he is feeling challenged and encouraged by his teachers."

One parent referred to the problems her child had while attending other schools and how the present school has changed everything:

"He is so happy and looks forward to going to school. He feels that he belongs at this school and he has been shown respect as an individual with talents and a mind of his own. [His] grades are above average and the changes are truly remarkable. If you were to read my son's last eight years of school history and then view my son in this school you would not believe it was the same child. The change is the most remarkable one I think you will find in this entire school. As a parent I love the fact I can walk into the classroom any time of day and sit down and see the learning process firsthand."

Another parent simply stated that the difference for her child was "there are no more tears." Imagine that going to school drives young people to tears. What does that say about a learning community? If we do nothing else, we ought to create the kinds of communities that value the joy of acceptance of self, the joy of being in a family of kindred spirits, and the joy of the wonderment of discovery. The voices of the students in the EdVisions schools speak eloquently to the fact that the Minnesota New Country School model can create such environments. In closing, a parent's comment is directed to all advisers, board members, support staff members, and all who have been involved in creating caring learning communities: "Thank you, thank you, thank you for all your hard work and creative vision!"

REFERENCES

Newell, R. (2003). *Passion for learning: How a project-based system meets the needs of 21st-century students*. Lanham, MD: Scarecrow Press.

Stoddard, L. (2003). *Educating for human greatness*. Brandon, VT: Holistic Education Press.

Afterword

Doug Thomas

Looking across the American educational landscape in 2004, I still don't see many of the kinds of schools being described in this book. I'm not sure we'll ever see enough of these schools. A national system of public education begs for structure, common curriculum, and conformity. What you've read here is not about those habits. We are unabashedly humanistic in our portrayal of what schools should be like in this relatively new century. We would like schools to be more humane not in an experimental or theoretical way but in a very practical sense. We want to see the relationships in schools strengthened so that a genuine trust develops between and among students, parents, and school staff. Our belief is that trust develops through authenticity, honesty, and purposeful values.

America is a confused country today, and especially so in its educational system. We as a country want more successful schools but can't define success in authentic ways. We want the public to support a public system that is defined and controlled by experts and bureaucrats who show little interest in the thoughts of educators, parents, or students. We want all of our students, no matter what ethnicity or ability, to achieve the same outcomes and possess the same skills. And we fail to agree on what values will be represented in the schools considered public. The latest round of top-down reforms leaves little room for discussion on any of these issues.

The former "farm kids with attitude" who started the New Country School and EdVisions Cooperative are struck with a "can do" attitude as they assist in the start-up of numerous other schools of likeness, despite the complicated issues being discussed in distant government agencies and state houses. Together with our colleagues and supporters, we represent hundreds of small groups who believe they can make a difference by making use of the good practices and research of those who have gone before us. That is the great thing about this nation. We can still dream and act on our dreams.

Yet the questions linger: Will these upstart groups be able to redefine public education for this century? Will the giant "system" squelch the innovations, the smallness and the independence of those who practice what they were taught to cherish about America? Will the entrepreneurial attitude, so highly valued in other sectors, support these folks during a long period of reinvention and reinvigoration? These questions are currently being answered and will continue to be answered during the coming decades.

For now, we need these small groups to move forward because of the wonderful things they are doing for our children. As is most obvious, this book was designed to send one strong message: "You can do this!" It was written for all those who have considered following their dreams but held back and for all those who let the "system" tell them "things would get better" or "next year you can create that innovative program." It was also for those who can't get rid of the nagging feeling that they could do better, who would provide additional time for the student who needs a bit more encouragement, and those who know they were "born to teach" but are restricted by the all too common rules and rigidity. It was written for all those teachers who want to do something extraordinary before they end their careers. At the same time, it was not written for those who want to be the boss, have a fight, or think that every day of this work is glamorous. It's hard, hard work—the most frustrating but exhilarating work you will ever experience in education!

What does it take to do this? After fifteen years of motivating, informing, and cajoling people to move forward with their dreams, I have found there are some key factors that must be in place in order to be successful, and despite the great ideas put forth in these prior chapters, there are some practical requirements that must be considered.

First, you must have a passion for teaching and learning in different ways. It is not enough to be a small school. Your school has to be a different, innovative school, trying new ideas. We are inadequate if we choose only to be a smaller version of what big schools have been practicing for decades. We lose that fight every time! And it's not that good for kids! We must take all the good research, student-centered activities, best practices, assessment strategies, and community-based learning and put them to work with students. These strategies must be the basis for creating a new learning program, not because we don't like the bureaucracy or our current principal or we want to make more money. We must strive for something better for young people and their families. It may seem obvious, but this is the foremost step in attracting a successful clientele for our new schools. Do something different!

Second, we must be given the autonomy to act on our dreams. The cruelest hoax played on teachers is the administration telling teachers to go ahead and create a new program and then undermining them by not giving them the professional authority to carry out a successful program. When I speak of autonomy, I mean all the decision making that will allow the program to thrive, including hiring and firing, policy development, school governance, and all the legal ramifications around student behavior and outcomes. This is often the shocker for most educators because they thought they would just be working with students. To carry out an innovative program, you must also have control over the design of that program. The innovation will be impossible if key control issues are left to someone else.

Third, those implementing the school must also have control of the money. The teachers could outsource for certain managerial functions, but redesign simply cannot take place without reallocation of funding. The school team must be given authority to determine how their public money is to be spent, including the rate of pay for teachers and how much administration is necessary and affordable. There are many ways to do this. The New Country School uses a teacher professional practice cooperative model. Others might create their own site management system or formal board. Performance pay and incentives must also be part of the picture. In any case, a key component is decisions regarding money allocation be made by those working with and being served by the school or program they create.

Fourth, the school must be willing to be accountable for results. If we are not able to stand up and say, "We did it differently and because of doing so, here's what we've been able to accomplish," we will come to nothing. This often goes far beyond test scores and standard measures. Parents want their children to be happy, active, and successful by a variety of measures. The public votes quite well with their feet these days. If we are a program of choice, parents often want more than the usual results.

There are several other features that could also be included in this listing, many that are mentioned in this book. Keeping your program or school small is very important, as are paying attention to parent and community involvement, service learning, and developing critical partnerships with businesses and organizations.

No matter how much work one does to ensure school success, the utmost attention must be paid to building a community both inside and outside the school building. As Walter Enloe, Darrol Bussler, James Lewicki, and others have pointed out so well, the establishment of a true learning community of adults and students will energize and sustain a group of well-intentioned folks beyond all the organizational, bureaucratic, and programmatic details. The ten years that the Minnesota New Country School has been in existence will be remembered not for its test scores or how they kept track of state standards but for the intellectual integrity of its teachers and the sense of community it created for its students and their families. The work of the new schools movement is in great part an opportunity for educators and the public to come together about something better, more meaningful, and more responsive. People don't easily come together anymore. It's takes a powerful community to satisfy the economic, social, educational, and political needs necessary to break away from the status quo. Schools like New Country are all about building community in real ways so young people can practice being part of a community.

We can no longer simply call a good school a "learning community." It is more complicated than just saying "this is a place where everyone learns together." It has to be a place that creates a culture of communal learning, but it also must acknowledge personalized learning in isolation as well. It has to be a setting that is attractive to many types of learners, a student-friendly place of comfort and accessible technology, and a schedule and program that respects both cooperative and independent learning.

It ought to be a mix of flexibility and structure along with a great deal of personal relevancy. It will be a community that can accept and serve a senior student who can't read along with a sophomore who knows exactly what he or she wants and can score a 30 on the ACT exam. Every school that groups students together in vague descriptions and assumptions has already lost its opportunity to create a true learning community. A true learning community is one where the adults agree to the premise that students are accepted for who they are and where they are and commit to helping them become successful.

In the broader community, the sense of hope and promise of public education has to be at least one of acceptance, if not outright support. Whether in a large urban area or a remote rural area, a portion of the immediate population must acknowledge the public nature of its schools. The community must be intentional. The schools should not exist by what Ted Kolderie of Education Evolving calls the "default arrangement," whereby if the doors are open and the kids keep coming, the school exists.

We're at a critical crossroad in the history of education in this nation. Charter schools like New Country represent the reinvention or reindependence of public schooling. Whether the community we serve accepts this evolution is very important to the survival of the notion of free public schooling and schooling for the common good. School choice and the latest round of accountability edicts may very well transform public education into a quasi-public entity. If the "last act of a dying institution is to make more rules," then we are surely on our last legs as a truly publicly sponsored system. Like the giant department stores of a generation ago, public schools may be in for a long slow ride into the sunset. Without community support, both financial and otherwise, it surely will look different in ten or twenty years.

The folks at EdVisions decided to get a head start on things. They became leaders on the front end of the new schools movement. Looking back at the chapters of this book, they have a road map of where they want to go. School by school, there must be new leadership. We believe that teacher–leaders need to step up and follow their dreams. Roland Barth, in his book, *Learning by Heart* (2001), speaks of teacher leadership as the necessary component to critical learning changes. He says, "The lives of teachers who lead are enriched and ennobled in many significant ways.

Rather than remain passive recipients, even victims of what their institutions deal to them, teachers who lead help shape their schools and, thereby, shape their own destinies as educators" (82). True professionals shape their own destinies and "generate students who are capable of both leading and learning" (82).

This book is a testament to teacher leadership and challenging the status quo. Our friend and colleague Joe Graba of Education Evolving says that "the schools we need cannot be created by fixing or changing the schools we currently have." We owe a tremendous debt of gratitude for those leading us and daring us to believe that we can re-create public schools. It is yet to be seen whether the schools being created by EdVisions will fuel the fires of reform or flicker and be snuffed out in a storm of institutional malaise. It is certain that a passionate dedication to student interests and deep learning will survive. Here is an example:

A student from the New Country School recently came to me with a request for financial assistance with his senior project. He was organizing what he called "An Evening of Elegance." He and several other students were doing a fund-raiser for the Leukemia Society. (His sister died last year of leukemia.) He was impressive in his appeal, and we gave him a modest amount. The young man was the overall organizer and fund-raiser for the event. Another senior student who was in culinary school through a postsecondary option program was preparing the entire meal for fifty people. Another was directing a one-act play to be presented after the meal. And yet another was showing clips from a local social history video she was producing.

The students did an impressive job with the entire event. Everything went off without a hitch. The event raised enough money to pay all the expenses, so all the ticket money was donated to the Leukemia Society. It was followed up with a very gracious, well-written thank you letter and an accounting of the proceeds and donation.

As I thought about what the students had done, I couldn't help but recall Joe Nathan's "six elements that most excite and motivate students":

- Education takes place out of the school building.
- Students really want to do it and have a choice in what they pursue.
- Students have an opportunity to collaborate with others.
- Students produce something for an audience beyond the teacher.

- Students' efforts are useful to other people.
- Students have an opportunity for reflection and refinement.

Aren't kids amazing when we give them a chance? The "coolest schools" tend to do that!

REFERENCE

Barth, R. (2001). *Learning by heart*. San Francisco: Jossey-Bass.

Index

About the Editors

Doug Thomas, M.S., spent a number of years as an outreach coordinator with the Center for School Change at the Humphrey Institute in Minneapolis. He is a graduate of Bemidji State College and has a master's in educational leadership from Minnesota State University in Mankato. He was the driving force behind the creation of the Minnesota New Country School and EdVisions Cooperative. He has been the director of the Gates–EdVisions Project since the reception of the Bill and Melinda Gates Foundation grant to replicate the New Country School and EdVisions model. He is a strong supporter and spokesperson for small schools, chartered schools, and rural education.

Walter Enloe, Ph.D., is a teacher for Hamline University's Graduate School of Education. From age twelve to seventeen, he lived in Japan, and after graduating from Eckerd College and Emory University, he taught grades K–12 at the Paideia School in Atlanta and was principal and teacher at the Hiroshima International School from 1980 to 1988. He has since been involved in a number of global studies and international peace initiatives in the education realm. He has been a consultant with EdVisions since 2000.

Ron Newell, Ed.D., taught high school history and social studies for twenty-five years in a traditional school, then helped Doug Thomas and others create the Minnesota New Country School and EdVisions Cooperative. He graduated from St. Olaf College, Minnesota State University–Mankato, and the University of South Dakota. After spending four years in higher education, he is presently working with the replication efforts of the Gates–EdVisions Project. Dr. Newell is the author of *Passion for Learning: How Project-Based Learning Meets the Needs of 21st-Century Students* (2003) and coauthor of *Democratic Learning and Leading: Creating Collaborative Governance* (2004), both by ScarecrowEducation.